Roger Harvey was born in Cornwall. He was educated in Newlyn and Falmouth before becoming a Cornwall Constabulary police cadet at the age of fifteen. On his retirement from the Devon and Cornwall Constabulary he became an animal health inspector for Cornwall County Council.

He now resides in North Devon and spends most of his time with his riding shire named "Jaunty" and in the preparation of young horses for their future roles in life.

HARVEY'S LAW

ROGER HARVEY

HARVEY'S LAW

Vanguard Press

VANGUARD PAPERBACK

© Copyright 2015
Roger Harvey

A CIP catalogue record for this title is
available from the British Library.

ISBN: 978-1-84386-964-1

Vanguard Press is an imprint of
Pegasus Elliot Mackenzie Publishers Ltd.

www.pegasuspublishers.com

First Published in 2015

Vanguard Press
Sheraton House Castle Park
Cambridge England
Printed & Bound in Great Britain

CHAPTER 1

It was a cold Monday morning in February when I left my family home at Gwavas as a fifteen-year-old and started the long walk to Newlyn Bridge, from where I was to catch the bus to Penzance. I wanted to turn up the collar of my overcoat but I wasn't sure if this was permitted as I was wearing the uniform of a Cornwall Constabulary police cadet. This was to be my first day on duty at the Penzance police station. As I sat on the bus, I reflected on things with a heavy heart. My desire had been to continue at school and then go on to study veterinary science. My father had plotted a very different career for me and in my life. I had learned it was in my best interests not to disagree with him.

I should describe the two men I knew as Father: the first had served in the Second World War and on his return, worked in the Newlyn fish trade as a buyer. He was a genial and well-liked member of the local community. The other one, residing in the four walls of our small home, was a glowering, violent presence to both my mother and me.

I had been attending the Newlyn infant school for two years when my father returned from the War and from the first day of his return, I was terrified of him. He always referred to me as 'boy' and never used my Christian name. He was a powerfully built man and whilst in the army was the regiment's light heavyweight boxing champion for four consecutive years.

On his return from service, my mother was immediately banned from showing any outward love towards me. When at home he spent his entire time coiled and ready to strike. The dropping of a knife or fork or a cough at the meal table also resulted in a cuff across the side of the head. Several times as a seven- and eight-year-old, I had stood in front of my mother in the kitchen, trying to protect her from one of his violent outbursts, with both of us in tears and terrified.

On one occasion, he decided that the shape of my nose should be changed, and for a few minutes over a week, I had to stand in front of him and made to pull my nose in a downward direction.

A regular visitor to the fish market was a Mr James, the village police constable and, unbeknownst to me, Constable James and my genial-in-public father were planning my future. I was exactly fifteen years of age when my father dropped the bombshell. He informed me that the chief inspector of Penzance police station would be calling that evening to inspect my school work with a view to my becoming a police cadet. I vainly protested but that, he said, was an end to it.

That evening, I was introduced to Chief Inspector Keast, after which my future was established with great speed. I was accepted into the Cornwall constabulary and after a medical and a uniform fitting at the police headquarters, I was given my posting to Penzance.

As a child, I had spent a great deal of time on my aunt and uncle's farm, which was a short walk from my home. I loved looking after the animals and both my aunt and uncle, who had no children of their own, took great delight in teaching me animal husbandry. I looked forward greatly to the farm visits where I would spend most of my time with the three working shire horses. Lucy was a jet-black mare aged fourteen and was only used for a bit of light work. The two geldings, a dapple-grey called Greybird, and Robin, a bay with four white legs, were the plough horses and general labourers. I was allowed to ride one and lead the other to and from the fields. I developed a great affinity with them.

Around this period, farms in the area were becoming mechanised, mainly with a little grey tractor. 'The Ferguson'. My uncle wasn't the least bit interested in tractors as he had his horses and that was that. My aunt, however, felt very differently and kept on at him to 'get on with the times'. My uncle finally yielded and agreed to the purchase of a new Ferguson which Frank, the farm labourer, named Jimmy. Whilst my uncle carried on working his beloved horses Frank drove Jimmy. It took my aunt a further six months of conscientious persistence to get my uncle to concede his traditional ground and agree to take driving lessons from Frank.

On a bright May morning and amidst much excitement and jollity, we all trundled off to the gently sloping grass field in which Uncle was to endure his first lesson. Frank made a great play of explaining several times the machine's controls, after which Uncle climbed aboard and with the engine already running, he for some unknown reason selected top gear and pulled the throttle right back, thus causing the tractor to career off down the slope. The tractor gathered speed at an alarming rate and, despite the efforts of shouting by Frank, the tractor carried on regardless. Just before the machinery ploughed into the hedge on the far side of the field, we could hear Uncle shouting, "Whoa, boy, whoa, whoa." And that was the first and last time Uncle sat on a tractor seat. My aunt never again mentioned the need to 'get with the times' and Uncle continued to work the land with his trusty horses until his retirement.

On the Sunday evening, the day before I was due to start at Penzance police station, I was on the Penzance promenade with a group of other lads, as was the practice to all meet up after compulsory church service. Large numbers of girls and boys had, over the years, paraded up and down the promenade after evening chapel or church services and many marriages came out of these meetings.

In our group we were laughing at the antics of one of the boys who was showing off to some girls, when I noticed a policeman watching us from the side of the road. I pointed this out to my group, who all turned to look at the constable.

The next thing I knew the constable crossed the road very quickly and grabbed hold of my tie and yanked me away from the rest of the group. I didn't resist – just felt stupid. The constable said, "Were you lot taking the micky out of me?"

I muttered, "No."

He released me and said, "Make sure you lot behave."

I got back to my group, who were all laughing or grinning and I could only think he picked on me because I was the tallest in the group.

The first person I encountered on entering the police station was the constable I had met on the promenade the previous evening.

"I recognise you," he said.

"We met last night, sir," I replied.

"You were in that group laughing at me," he said.

I tried to say something, thinking this was not a good start, when he stuck out his hand and we shook hands.

"I'm not 'sir', but Sam, OK?" he said.

So it was that Police Constable 327 Samuel George Matthews and I became friends.

Many years later we were both stationed at Truro, I would remind him of the time he assaulted me on the Penzance promenade.

Chief Inspector Keast made me very welcome and so my life in the force began.

CHAPTER 2

My parents had now moved from the area and I was living with my grandparents in Penzance and was well and truly involved in the life at the Penzance police station.

I was getting on well with the other constables, one in particular called Harry Deal. Harry was a man that few would argue with as his presence often quelled a disturbance. He encouraged me to swim with him on summer mornings from the Penzance promenade before the start of duty. He played water polo and would rear up out of the sea like a whale and hurl the ball straight at you with a shout and then disappear under the waves and surface somewhere completely different.

All the station staff appeared to get on well with each other and amusing stories of happenings on the different shifts could heard being related at the end of their tours.

One morning a beat constable, called Johnny, who was blessed with a girth of a shire horse, was called up before the chief inspector to explain his lack of effort in respect of an incident at the Penzance railway station the previous evening. Apparently, two young men had messed with the porter's trolley and removed goods from another. The constable had been in the police box (*Dr Who* TARDIS) outside the railway station when he received a complaint but was too slow to react due to his size. The chief inspector's door was slightly ajar and I was able to hear what was being said.

"If you couldn't catch them in time, why didn't you blow your whistle?" asked the chief inspector.

"I did, sir," replied the constable.

"What happened?"

"The train went out, sir."

I very nearly burst out laughing and had to move away from the door. I don't know what else was said but I bet it would have been worth listening to.

In those days, constables attended all post-mortems and one particular day there was no one to attend a post-mortem that day and I was to go to the local hospital and watch the proceedings for continuity.

I arrived at the hospital to find that Dr Hocking, the regular pathologist, was on holiday and there was a stand-in. On entering the mortuary, I saw a very obese lady on the slab. A lump came into my throat and I knew that I wasn't going to enjoy what was coming next. The pathologist took out the heart, liver and lungs, followed by the brain of the deceased. By this time I was beginning to feel sick and covered my nose with a handkerchief. There seemed to be blood everywhere and I wanted it all to be over.

The pathologist looked puzzled and then took out the intestines. He turned to me and said, "Would you hold this end a moment?" He handed me the intestines, which he then stretched out across the mortuary and proceeded to slice with scissors. After a few moments he let out an "aha," followed by, "There is the answer, young man, blood in the intestine."

One of the first duties I had to undertake was to write down, in longhand, all telephone messages from Divisional Headquarters at Camborne. Several times a day operational or wanted descriptions had to be recorded. Having taken a message it then had to be typed and placed on the station log. I found that most of my day was consumed with this chore, so I decided to take evening shorthand/typing classes. I commenced the course with 'Miss Wesley's School of Typing'. The school was based in an old Victorian building in the centre of Penzance.

On my first evening class, I found myself the only male with a dozen females. We sat on chairs facing tables, which in turn faced the walls around the room. The typewriters had a wooden screen over the keys with just enough space for one's hands to operate the keys. This completely mystified me but I could eventually see the merit of it if you wanted to touch type.

Today, I can still smell the gas lamps that burned on the walls mixed with the girls' cheap perfume which readily became available after the War.

It was, however, worth the effort as I spent less time on the station's clerical work.

CHAPTER 3

The Penzance motorcycle patrol officer, who was a bit of a lad, was often seen arriving at Penzance police station with someone he had arrested on the pillion seat of his machine.

The Penzance sub-division had quite a good cricket team and, at times, when there weren't enough constables available to make up the eleven, I would be pulled in to play. On one particular occasion, we were due to play St Just on their ground. As per usual, we set off in the sergeant's cars. As we arrived at the cricket field in St Just village, the car I was riding in was being driven by a sergeant who was not the most popular man, with his men or the public, and as he drove through the field gate the half-shaft on the car broke. The car was pushed into the field and the game got underway. When the match was over, a farmer who played for St Just came over and the sergeant explained the situation. The farmer offered to tow the car back to Penzance and the sergeant readily accepted.

The farmer's car was a new Jaguar. I went to get into the sergeant's car when the farmer asked if I had ever ridden in a Jaguar. When I replied, "No," he invited me to ride with him and the sergeant agreed to this.

After a mile or so, the farmer started to increase his speed, so much that I could hear the sergeant sounding his horn. I glanced back and could see the sergeant with one hand on the steering wheel and the other waving frantically. I informed the farmer who, in turn, informed me that he'd been waiting for years to get the bastard, adding, "And now I've got him for what he did to me. He obviously didn't recognise me."

The terror ride continued until we reached a crossroads on the outskirts of Penzance, where the Jaguar braked suddenly. The sergeant, not ready for this, pulled his car out and passed the Jaguar, breaking the tow rope in the manoeuvre. Fortunately we were the only vehicles at the crossroads as the sergeant and his car disappeared from sight down Newlyn Combe.

The farmer kindly dropped me off at home and as I thanked him, he said it had been well worth it. I didn't see the sergeant for several days and when I did, the incident was not mentioned, which was a relief to me.

There were just a handful of policewomen in the county in the 1950s and a rather delightful girl was stationed at Penzance. This was her first posting and she was in her first year of the probationary period of two years. On one particular briefing, Dorothy was advised by the duty sergeant to produce a few more traffic offences. After briefing, Dorothy set off down Market Jew Street ready for action and almost immediately spotted an ice cream van stationary, with the driver serving ice cream from the side window. To Dorothy's delight, the engine of the van was running. This would be her first offence of the day, 'engine left running when driver not in attendance'. Dorothy waited patiently until the last person was served and then approached the ice cream salesman. Dorothy pointed out the offence and asked to see the man's driving licence and insurance. The man obliged and listened as Dorothy informed him he was being reported for the offence committed. By now several people were waiting to be served. The ice cream man hadn't stopped smiling since Dorothy had approached his van and in fact, hadn't said a word, but now he got out of the van and pointed to the running motor which was working to keep his refrigerator cool. He then indicated that the engine of the van was off, the noise was coming from the refrigeration motor. Dorothy never did say what she said to the ice cream man but did admit her face felt red for the rest of the tour of duty.

One morning, I was taken by the duty sergeant to Newlyn to spend a few hours on tour with PC James to give me an insight into a country constable's work.

Constable James lived in a police house in the centre of the village and was coming to the end of his service, most of which had been in Newlyn village, so he was well known.

The locals referred to him affectionately as 'Dick Barton', the special agent who could be heard on the radio each week. Two of my mates were cycling over Newlyn Bridge one dark evening when one said, "I don't see Dick Barton anywhere."

A voice from the doorway of the butcher's shop said, "I'm over here." So Mr James was well aware of his nickname.

The duty sergeant made a quick introduction of me to Constable James, then departed after advising me that I would be picked up a couple of hours later.

Mr James always stood ramrod straight, his iron-grey hair cut short and he talked with a nasal twang. He was well respected by the community at large and feared by those he pursued.

His greeting to me was, "Well, Mr Harvey, we have work to do," and with that we set off on foot up the Newlyn Coombe along the river bank, with the intention of reaching a meadow to serve a summons on a Gypsy type of man who lived in a caravan in the meadow. A short distance up the Coombe, we passed the Gaiety Cinema and Mr James nodded towards it and asked if it was one of my haunts. I replied it was and reminded him of a night many months before when he was called to the cinema to quell a major disturbance.

The first dozen row of seats were the 'ten penny' seats and separated from these seats by a low wall was the main body of seats, accessed by a staircase. The 'one shilling and nine pence' seats. The cinema was privately owned by a Mr and Mrs Flower who drove a Triumph May Flower car.

On this particular Saturday, I was with my mates in the 'ten pencers' and in the intermission, a Newlyn boy called Sammy Hitchens, climbed up onto the stage in front of the film screen and shouted, "Mr Flower has said all these ten pencers can sit in the one and nines."

Chaos erupted as all the boys in the front seats climbed over the wall into the one and nines. Mr Flower attempted to get everyone back but to no avail. It took the presence of Constable James to restore normality during which time Sammy Hitchens had disappeared.

We had now reached the meadow and were greeted by a fierce barking from a wolf type of dog, chained to the wheel of a caravan some one hundred yards away from us. The caravan door was flung open and a bearded man in his fifties appeared at the opening. The man shouted, "Bugger off, or I will release the dog."

Mr James replied, "I have a summons for you, which will be served."

The man then carried on cursing and, seeing no police retreat, released the dog which came bounding towards us. Mr James swept me behind him with his arm, drew his truncheon, and held it parallel at chest height with his hands at each end. The dog was now only feet away and, seeing the truncheon held in front of the constable, leapt for it and clenched his teeth onto the centre of the truncheon. Mr James then, with great force, brought his knee up into the dog's heart and the dog, with a gasp, fell lifeless to the ground.

The summons was duly served and we walked back down the Coombe and onto the pier to look at the fishing fleet. By the time the duty sergeant arrived I was feeling a little stunned by what I had witnessed. In later life, whilst playing with my own dogs, I have held a stick or rod as demonstrated that day and found that they will always jump for it.

CHAPTER 4

One morning during the sitting of the Penzance quarter sessions, when most of the station staff were at the court, Dorothy and I were the only ones in the station. Dorothy disappeared for a few minutes and reappeared dressed in one of the constable's motorcycle breeches, crash helmet, goggles and gloves. At that time I was using a bumper to polish the long wooden floor of the corridor which ran through the middle of the station. The bumper was a two feet square wood block to which was attached a long handle with a folded blanket under the block which, when pulled, buffed the wooden floor. The station cleaner was on holiday so the job had fallen to me.

Dorothy was laughing and got on the bumper, holding on to the handle like a jockey. I immediately started off down the corridor towing Dorothy on the bumper and made a couple of runs, each time getting faster. On the final run, as we reached the end of the corridor, Dorothy went to jump off but misjudged and landed in a heap right in front of Chief Inspector Keast, who had, at that moment, returned from court to collect some papers. I was dismissed and Dorothy was taken into the chief inspectors office for a dressing down in more ways than one.

At times my duties would be altered and I would work the two p.m. till ten p.m. shift. On one of these shifts, the country station sergeant called to collect me from the Penzance police station. He was going to the Newlyn Gaiety Cinema to inspect the seating and fire appliances. It turned out that he also wanted to see the last part of the film that he had missed on a previous occasion.

For many years, my grandmother had a cat called Billy, who died of old age. I asked if she would like another to replace Billy. The answer was yes so I picked up Fluffy, one of the farm cats, but Fluffy had different ideas about being a town cat. The first thing that Fluffy did was to tear around the house, jump on the mantelpiece and proceed to knock off the ornaments, so she went back to the farm and Grandmother settled for a blue budgie.

I was enjoying my time in Penzance but had a shock when a memo arrived from the chief constable's office, informing me I was going to be posted to police headquarters at Bodmin with immediate effect. Cadets normally remained in the same station they had originally been posted to until doing National Service or becoming a constable.

My grandparents were very sad at my departure, as was

the girl I had been seeing on a regular basis from the village of Mousehole.

A wind of change was blowing through headquarters as the old chief constable, Major Hare, had retired and Mr R B Matthews had taken over.

CHAPTER 5

A training department had been formed, headed by an inspector and a sergeant, and it was this department that instigated cadets from divisions to be posted to headquarters and placed in various departments. We were also allocated places at various lodging houses in Bodmin town and I, with two others, shared an attic room in a large house.

My first attachment was to the traffic department, which was headed by an inspector and two sergeants. The only drawback to being stationed at headquarters was the ridiculous routines we were put through at certain times of the week by the training inspector and his sergeant, who soon got the name of 'Bilko'. The inspector used to take us each week for a foot drill at Bodmin army barracks, where he would shout commands at us and, believe it or not, he would carry a regimental sergeant major's pace stick. One day, after a period of marching, I returned to the traffic office feeling a bit dejected when one of the motor patrol sergeants asked me what was wrong. I vented my feelings about the antics of the inspector and, to my surprise, the sergeant started to laugh and said, "I was in the same regiment as him in the army. He couldn't march to save his soul and was called 'The Sugar Plum Fairy' by the regimental sergeant major."

The clothing store at headquarters was run by a sergeant who had done the job for many years and had been allocated a cadet for a period of training. A force inspection by HM Inspector was shown the clothing department by the chief constable and his staff officers. The HM inspector, on seeing the cadet on parade, asked him what he did. The cadet, who was known as a bit of a talker, launched into a great speech of what he did. The HM inspector then turned to the sergeant and said, "What do you do, sergeant?"

He said, "I assist the cadet, sir." The tension was immediately broken and a few smiles broke out.

There were two typists in the traffic office, one of which kept a photograph of Dirk Bogarde on the wall beside her desk. I don't know what possessed me but one day, when I was in the office on my own, I drew a moustache on poor old Dirk. The next day all hell broke loose when it was discovered that Dirk had grown a moustache. I had to own up and was nearly skinned alive. How was I to know she was in love with Dirk?

After a few months, I was moved from the traffic department to headquarters CID, where in the first week I saw photographs of a double murder scene. This was the first time colour photography had been used to record a murder in the county.

A daily duty of all headquarters' cadets, was to take the morning tea and biscuits into the chief constable's office, which he then shared with the deputy chief constable. A new cadet called Frank arrived and we immediately informed him that it was his week for tea duty to the chief constable. Frank was eager to do the job and make a good impression in front of the chief. He was instructed to collect the silver tray from the kitchen, where it had been prepared by the cook, take off his tunic and roll up his sleeves and upon arriving at the chief's door, to knock smartly and enter. Once inside, place the tray on the chief's polished table, then about turn and march out. Frank left the kitchen with the tray, with his sleeves rolled up, and showing a beautiful pair of army braces over his blue shirt.

On entering the chief's office, Frank saw both the chief and his deputy in conversation, which ended at the sight of Frank in his braces, followed by a roar from the deputy to have the hot tray removed from the polished table. Frank did not forget this unfortunate episode or forgive us.

Nineteen years of age at last and sworn in as Constable 22, I was away to Chantmarle Training Centre in Dorset and began a twelve week course of intensive training. Definitions, powers of arrest and numerous other things to be learnt off by heart. We marched for a period each day to band music on a record player. We also had unarmed combat, physical training, cross country and, for the

Cornish who didn't go home at weekends, fire drill.

My time at Chantmarle was quite uneventful apart from watching the antics of a probationary constable from the Bristol City force. In civil life, he had been a part time stand-up comedian. A lot of the new recruits were ex-servicemen who paraded with their medals. One day, the comedian appeared on parade with a row of medal ribbons on his tunic. What he had done was to take a lolly stick and carefully stuck Spangle sweet wrappers around it, making it look exactly like four medal ribbons. He wore them for over a week before an instructor noticed.

I heard over the grapevine that he didn't survive a year in the job as he was asked to resign after delivering a death message to a lady whose husband had been killed in a road accident. He apparently greeted the lady by saying, "Good morning, Widow Brown."

The building at Chantmarle was surrounded by a moat and it was this water that fed the fire pump with which we practised at weekends. During the time I spent there, no emergency arose.

A constable from Dorset was asked by a class instructor what he would do in relation to a set of circumstances that he encountered on patrol.

As the constable was passing a pub, a man staggered out clutching a knife stuck in his chest, followed by several people fighting, one of whom falls into the road and under a car which runs over his leg. The driver, you can see, is under the influence of drink. By this time a large crowd has gathered. What action would you take?

The constable paused for a moment, looked at the class instructor, and said, "I would take my helmet off, sir, and mingle with the crowd." Everyone in class burst out laughing.

Whilst at Chantmarle, my posting came through for Newquay. It was August 1959 and Newquay was packed with visitors. I was billeted in Newquay police station in a bedroom, shared with two other constables, immediately above the charge room. The bedroom floor had bare floorboards, iron bedsteads, no wardrobes but a picture rail to hang clothes on. The Criminal Investigation Department office was also on the first floor, immediately opposite the bedroom door. Further along the passage was a room for two more constables.

The station inspector was Mr Cole, who was quite aloof from the constables and who could make you feel inadequate at times. There were two sergeants, one of which was Sergeant Craig, known as 'Busty', who when I was a cadet at headquarters was one of the motor patrol sergeants.

Most of us played tennis in the summer and tried to get a match in at least two or three times a week. Busty, who was twice the age of most of us, always boasted that when he hit the ball, he hit it so hard that when it passed over the net it went oval shaped. He tried his best but could never beat the youngsters.

He was remonstrating with a group of Hells Angels once when one of the group challenged him on his knowledge of motorcycling. Busty, in his normal style, described how, in the War, he had crossed a desert riding his motorcycle whilst asleep. There was no answer to that and a few mouths were left open as he walked away.

On my day off one week, I was going to catch the train to travel home to see my mother and was just about to leave the police station when Inspector Cole entered the doorway. He asked me where I was going and I explained. He asked me when my train left and when I told him, he said, "That's over an hour away. The front step of the station needs a good clean, you can do that before you leave." There was never any questioning or refusing Mr Cole.

I was on nine a.m. till six p.m. charge room duty one day when my mother, to my surprise, came into the station, having caught a bus to Newquay to drop some shirts in for me as I hadn't been home for some time. We talked for a couple of minutes when the inspector's door opened and Inspector Cole came out. "Who's this, Harvey?" he asked.

I explained.

"If you would like to take half an hour off to speak to your mother, you can, providing you come on duty from midnight to make up for it." Mother fled the station and never visited me again at Newquay in all the time I was stationed there.

CHAPTER 6

During the summer months all sorts came to Newquay and invariably when checking a person sleeping rough, you would find that a warrant had been issued somewhere in the UK or the person was wanted for questioning in connection with a criminal offence. After two a.m., there would only be two constables on duty, one manning the station and the other on foot patrol. As there was no way of communicating with the station other than the telephone kiosk, you would normally walk the suspect to the station and from there telephone the criminal record office. If there was no record, then the person would be given a cup of tea and sometimes be allowed to spend a few hours in the single men's restroom before being sent on their way at six a.m.

I checked a chap sleeping in a bus shelter at four thirty a.m. one morning and took him in for a check. He wasn't wanted so was given a cup of tea in the restroom. I carried on with my night patrol, leaving the constable to send the chap on his way when he had finished his tea. I finished my tour of duty at six a.m., climbed the stairs to bed and dropped off to sleep. The next thing I knew, I was being woken by the duty sergeant who told me to get dressed in my uniform as Inspector Cole wanted to see me immediately. It was eight a.m. and I had been in bed less than two hours.

Apparently, my night shift colleague had forgotten to turn the chap out and he was found at seven thirty a.m. by the early turn constable who then sent him on his way. A short while after, Inspector Cole had come into the station (he lived in a police house at the front of the station) and asked if anyone had seen his cat. The lady station cleaner piped up, "I expect the man who was looking in your dustbin took your cat."

Under interrogation from the inspector, the duty constable revealed everything. Hence my summons.

I was given a dressing down and dismissed. As I left the inspector's office, I very nearly tripped over his cat that had wandered in.

A few months later, Inspector Cole departed and Inspector John Osborne arrived with his two German shepherds. He encouraged me to give the dogs a run on the beaches in the winter. They were great company and Sabre, the youngest dog, was great for searching in caves. We didn't have a dog section in Cornwall in those days.

In the early sixties, trains brought people from all parts of the country to Newquay, especially when the big factories closed for their annual holidays. In addition to holidaymakers, Newquay had on its doorstep RAF St Mawgan and Penhale army camp. To cover the eastern end of the town in the evening there would be patrolling from six p.m. to two a.m. As I mentioned, after two a.m. there would only be one constable on patrol. As there were only two sergeants, the sergeant would invariably finish by midnight and from there on would be on call. The Blue Lagoon dance hall on the eastern end would be the big attraction and with the RAF, army and visitors, there would be numerous outbreaks of fights and fierce arguments, mainly over young women, fuelled of course by drink.

For a while we were plagued by groups of Hells Angels creating havoc, but they stopped visiting the town because someone kept putting sugar in the petrol tanks. This was the secret weapon of Sergeant Craig, who enlisted me to aid and abet him; it was great crime prevention!

I had become engaged to Pamela, a girl from Mousehole, but had noticed a large number of foreign girls coming to Newquay to work in the hotels and restaurants. They all had, on arrival, to report to Newquay police station with passports and work permits. I think it was at this time I realised I was far too young to be married and called off the engagement. I felt a bit of a rotter in doing so but knew it was the right thing to do.

I became attracted to a young Swiss girl called Esther, who worked at the Sussex Grill as a waitress and we became friends. When working the six p.m. to two a.m. shift, Esther would, after the grill closed, look for me and provide me with a bit of chicken which was, as a single man, great because at that age one is always hungry. I used to keep the offering under my cape until it was safe to eat.

One night, just as the local chip shop was closing, I nipped in and bought some fish and chips and slipped them under my cape until I found somewhere quiet to eat them. I started to walk down the street when I was approached by the duty sergeant. He took me on what I can only describe as a route march for about an hour and as he left me he said, "Goodnight, you can eat your chips now." I had to bin them.

A pay review had taken place and senior constables were to get a thousand pounds a year after some twenty years' service and my increase from that of a cadet to a constable permitted me to buy a secondhand Austin Cambridge car. This was ideal for my courtship of Esther but also led to an embarrassing incident. I had collected Esther after midnight from her work and we drove to a secluded car park just outside Newquay in the countryside. We got carried away and both ended up completely naked in the car. I thought I had locked all the doors but had omitted to secure the front passenger door. I was completely taken by surprise when the door was pulled open and a torch flashed over our naked bodies. A voice I immediately recognised said, "Oops, sorry, Rog." It was the village constable, Police Constable Waters, in whose beat area I was parked. It certainly killed our passion that night. But give him his due, he didn't let on to anyone else what he had seen.

At the end of that summer, Esther stayed in Newquay to help at the local Doctor Barnardo's Home, where, when required, I helped out also. It was very rewarding at times.

CHAPTER 7

Opposite Newquay police station in East Street where at the front of the station the inspector and sergeant lived and, as I have already mentioned, the five single constables resided, there was John Julian's Furniture Store. One night the safe in the store was dynamited and nobody heard it. Fortunately, a few weeks later a man was arrested and convicted for the crime.

Inspector Osborne was instrumental in getting our bedroom an upgrade. We were to have new beds, wardrobes and canvas on the floor. The day came for our new furnishings to arrive and I and another constable, Doug, were detailed to remove all the old beds and a chest of drawers. The easiest way was to lower everything out of the large bedroom window into the courtyard below and then to be carried to the bottom of the garden. I did the lowering but after several walks to the bottom of the garden, Doug complained and wanted to change over so that he did the lowering and I did the walking. I agreed, but before he came upstairs, we arranged to have a cup of tea.

In the meantime, I got a chest of drawers balanced on the window ledge and had filled the drawers with some of my barbell weights and had tied the lowering rope on. I went down the stairs, had my drink and we changed over. Before I could get out into the yard, the station's detective sergeant appeared and started to question me about a matter I had dealt with. His back was towards the large charge room window, immediately underneath the window we were using to lower the furniture. I was some six to eight feet away from the detective sergeant, facing the window. Suddenly, to my horror, I saw the chest of drawers come into sight and come to a halt and then crashed into the window behind the detective sergeant. He immediately dived under the charge room table shouting, "Christ. It's a bomb." In fact what had happened was that Doug managed to push the chest of drawers off the window not realising I had played a prank on him. He then jumped on the rope to stop it crashing into the courtyard, causing it to swing inwards. We were thankful that we were explaining what had happened to Inspector Osborne and not Inspector Cole!

Another amusing episode comes to mind in which one of the more senior constables, who should have known better, persistently visited the local hospital when on duty and would make a nuisance of himself with the nurses. I think he thought he was Cornwall's answer to Errol Flynn. Unfortunately, he had to go into hospital for a minor operation. The matron, who was a good sort and was wise to his behaviour with her nurses, took on the job of induction. He was advised that his temperature had to be taken via his anus in order to get an exact body temperature. He didn't question it and was told to go into a curtained cubicle, kneel on the bed with his trousers and pants down ready to have his temperature taken. Shortly after, the procedure was complete, or so he thought. Several weeks later, I was called to the hospital to take a road accident statement from a patient, after which I was offered a cup of tea by one of the nurses I knew fairly well. I was then sworn to secrecy and shown a photograph which was kept hidden in the nurses' room. The picture was of the constable kneeling on the bed with his naked bum in the air and sticking out of his anus was a daffodil.

On night duty, especially after midnight, you were expected to try all the door handles of the shops in the main street and quite often a door would be found unlocked. One morning, about three a.m., I was shaking hands with door knobs in Bank Street, Newquay and as I tried the door handle of a jeweller's shop, I shone my torch into the shop. As I did so, I saw a foot being withdrawn behind the counter. The door had a Chubb lock and there was no evidence of a break in to the front of the shop. I ran round to the back of the shop, climbed over the back wall and hoisted myself up onto the first floor flat roof just as a man leapt over me and fell into the yard below. A skylight on the roof was open and I could see signs of someone else coming up through it. As I got to the skylight, the head of another man appeared. I hauled him out and after a brief struggle managed to handcuff him and manhandled him down into the yard. There was no sign of the first burglar. The pockets of the chap were full of jewellery. I marched him up to the police station, took everything off him and put him in a cell. As luck would have it, a patrol car crew called into the station at that moment and volunteered to go back to the jeweller's to make a search for the missing offender. After twenty minutes or so, one of the motor patrol constables shouted from across the green. He had found the first man hiding in a tree. The fellow cannot have gone very far as he had injured an ankle in jumping off the roof. I was awarded a favourable record from the chief constable for that bit of duty.

I kept a set of weights under the charge room table which I used every day to keep fit and at times would hold power lifting challenges with any of the constables who wished to try their luck.

My father had, when we were living at Gwavas, also enlisted me in the army cadets and onto the boxing team. I became quite good at it as I didn't like getting hurt. I managed to do a bit of sparring at RAF St Mawgan and at the army camp at Penhale, both camps being in the Newquay police area.

One day, I was having lunch in the police station when one of the senior constables, dear old Sid Crick, who when talking on the telephone always spelt his surname out to the listener, called me up to the charge room and introduced me to a fairground boxing promoter. Sid explained that a fair was in the area for a couple of days and that they were looking for challengers. I said I wasn't interested until the promoter asked how much I earned per week. I believe it was around nine or ten pounds and the promoter said, "You can earn that for three rounds with one of our boys."

Sid egged me on and on the next evening, I found myself in the crowd with my 'second', PC Nick Mayne. As pre-arranged, the promoter came out of his boxing booth with a very big, burly champion and asked for a challenger. After a moment or so I put my hand up and the fight was on. It was agreed that I would get the better of my fellow pugilist in the first round and then he would win the second and we would draw in the third. I took a few heavy knocks and gave a few, after which I was given my money and Nick and I left as we were both on the night shift.

At about eleven p.m. that night, I was called to a disturbance outside the Central Hotel pub, in Central Square, involving four men who were the worse for wear through drink. I could see I was going to have my hands full and a large crowd had started to form and calls were egging the men on to fight. The street lights were good in this part of town and as I tried to get between the first pair, someone in the crowd flipped the back of my helmet, resulting in it falling off. I was now hatless, facing the first man at close range, pinning his arms at his side. He stared at me and I could see a look of surprise come over his face as he uttered, "You're the bloke who was boxing at the fair."

I saw my chance and replied, "Yes, so you all know what to expect." It was as if someone had waved a magic wand and hands were being shaken as I asked for everyone to move along or go home, which the majority, including my troublesome quartet, did.

An incident comes to mind where a motorcycle patrol officer was cleaning his police motorcycle. The machine was parked under the single quarters' window and as soon as the motorcycle was sparkling clean, one of the constables leaned out of the window and poured a bucket of water down over the machine. The motor patrol constable was fuming and shouted abuse at the culprit and started to clean the machine again, but as soon as he had finished the same thing happened again. This time he decided to move the machine away from its position under the bedroom window and for the third time began cleaning the motorcycle. He was beside himself with anger as his motorcycle was due for headquarters' inspection later that day.

The culprit had now got himself ready to go out for the day and was dressed in a smart suit and calmly walked out of the station into the yard where the still fuming constable was cleaning the motorcycle. Without warning, he picked up the bucket of dirty water and threw it over the culprit. He was covered from head to foot in dirty, oily water and the suit he was wearing was drenched. "It's OK," he said to the motor patrol constable, "because, you see, I've got your best suit on!"

There was quite a lot of respect for the police in the sixties and many times when on duty, I've called to a group of rowdies to quieten down or move on and a reply would come back, "Yes, sir" or "Sorry, officer." Riotous, drunken groups were a different matter and a visit to the cells had, more often than not, a sobering effect.

During the summer months, Newquay very often became gridlocked, causing a few motorists to lose their cool.

On one particular day, I was engaged on traffic duty at the eastern end of the town and attempting to get traffic out of the junction for those wishing to leave the town. Traffic on the main road in was at a standstill when a car horn started to sound intermittently some fifty cars back from me in the queue. I was able to identify the car and after a while it drew level with me and had to stop. The driver's window was open and the driver, who was accompanied by his wife and three teenage children, was staring straight ahead to avoid eye contact with me.

I bent down and peered into the car, but the driver still refused eye contact. His wife, however, looked embarrassed and glanced at me. I winked at her and then said, "Now, sir, if you would be so kind as to give me the second chorus of the Trumpet Voluntary, it will enable me to book you for sounding your horn while stationary, or alternatively, you could say 'sorry, constable' and accept a verbal caution."

The driver looked very serious but his wife and kids started to giggle, with his wife saying, "We apologise for him."

I said, "Apology accepted. Now drive on and enjoy your holiday." The traffic had started to move and some car lengths away I could see the teenagers still waving to me through the back window of the car.

Like any job, the police had tricks of the trade and one I used on night duty was where there was a dead end alley that I had checked, was to stretch a piece of cotton across the entrance of the alley and then later on the return patrol to check it. If it was broken, you knew immediately that it had to be checked again. If intact, it saved a journey. If you had time between points on patrol on night shift, especially if you were looking for someone in particular, you would check the canvas beach huts. On one occasion, I pulled back a canvas flap and my torch picked out a young man sitting in the single deckchair. His immediate reaction was to call out, "Standing room only." A right comedian.

A few prostitutes operated in Newquay in the sixties and one in particular, a very large girl, could be seen performing on the beach. Her name was 'Half Crown Annie' and she was well known to the service personnel.

There was always a funny side to most of the things you saw on patrol but also some sad happening. One afternoon a call was received at the station to the effect there were two young children in the lane at the back of Mount Wise, crying because they couldn't get into their home after school. I was sent to investigate and by the time I got there, a neighbour was looking after the children. I had a good look at the back of the terraced house and through a chink in the kitchen curtain saw the body of a woman lying in a pool of blood. A murder investigation was put into operation and a search made for the murdered woman's husband. Sadly, later that evening, his body was found washed up on the beach. The husband and wife were not young people and it was very sad for those left behind.

One of the single chaps that lived in the station was called Brian. He also came from Newlyn and, oddly enough, his father also worked in the fish trade. Brian was a couple of years older than me and played rugby and cricket for the county. He also played fast and loose with his women. He was engaged to a Newquay girl and at the same time going out with a rather beautiful German girl who worked at The Sussex Grill. When she returned to Germany at the end of the summer, Brian started going out with another Newquay girl whilst still engaged to number one. I had completed a two p.m. till ten p.m. shift one evening and gone to bed when, about midnight, I was woken up by Brian pleading with me to help him out. Apparently he had the girl he was engaged to outside the station in his white Austin A30 car and the other girl in the station professing her undying love for him. What he wanted me to do was drive number one to her home while he tried to pacify girl number two.

I dressed and went to his car where sat number one, and tried to mumble something but she didn't want to engage in small talk. I pleaded ignorance to what was going on. It was now approaching one a.m. as I pulled into the dark driveway of her home and came to a halt. For the second time in my life the driver's door was wrenched open and a fist slammed into me, at the same time number one screamed, "Dad, it's not Brian." The driveway was then floodlit and I got out of the car to see a bearded, hulking man. Number one, I found out, had phoned her father and informed him of Brian's other mistress, so he was waiting in the dark to sort him out. That was the last time I aided Brian and his women. As it happened, Brian resigned two years later – a great pity as apart from his women troubles, he was a great copper.

Other memories of Newquay were when some idiot put boot polish on the shop door handles and a constable coming to work in uniform and taking his helmet off without realising he still had hair grips in. His wife liked him with a quiff and had forgotten about the hair grips when he went off to work.

CHAPTER 8

I had now been at Newquay for three years and was very sorry to receive a posting to Wadebridge, a town further up the north Cornish coast. I had sold my car because it had become too costly to keep and Esther had returned to Switzerland.

With all my worldly possessions packed into two cases, I caught the bus to Wadebridge and as I gazed out of the window watching the countryside pass by, I had time to reflect on my time at Newquay.

I remember my first day on the beat, being called to a hotel in which a woman had fallen off a bar stool and died. I had conjured up all sorts in my mind such as, was she poisoned or had she taken an overdose? It turned out to be death from natural causes.

The man I had caught using his electric shaver from the bulb socket in a telephone kiosk, a straightforward case of fraudulent extraction of electricity, but could I only caution him as he stated he had seen a police constable doing the self-same thing and had just copied him.

My first case of depositing litter, where the offender refused to pick up his chip papers and was subsequently fined the equivalent of my week's wages.

I was jolted out of my thoughts as the bus came to a halt quite near the Wadebridge police station and I scrambled out and presented myself inside the building where I met the one and only Sergeant Frank Organ and Inspector W T G Cock. The rest of the staff was made up of a civilian typist, a CID constable and four uniform constables.

Sergeant Organ informed me that lodgings had been arranged for me with a Mrs Chope, whose guest house overlooked the railway station. Having lived in the Newquay police station for the past three years, I wasn't looking forward to moving back into lodgings, but there was no alternative but to grin and bear it. I was welcomed by Mrs Chope and soon introduced to my fellow lodgers, a retired customs officer, a SWEB clerical worker, an egg packer who was also a local preacher, a two-year-old boy and a very attractive bank clerk called Angela.

Wadebridge was completely different from the hustle and bustle of Newquay. There would be only one constable on duty at any one time and the three regular shifts worked gave twenty-four hour coverage, therefore night shift came around every three weeks, whereas at Newquay it had been every four weeks.

After my first week of duty, I soon learned about two young men from families who regarded themselves as the hard men of the town. They were hard drinkers and gave the police officer who would have been on duty a hard time, especially when the public houses were closing. They had been allowed to carry on with their bad behaviour without ever having been taken to task. Having been working the beat at Newquay for the last three years, where we carried out a zero policy towards violence, I wasn't particularly worried about what I was going to come across. I had quite a bit of experience in boxing and self-defence and had been called upon several times, even when off duty, to sort out problems of violence.

On my third week of duty, I found myself having to deal with a fight in the town hall, where a dance was being held. I soon discovered that the two men previously mentioned were the cause of the disturbance. They had got into the dance hall without payment and were attempting to help themselves to free booze. With the help of a couple of hefty lads, I got them outside and warned them about their conduct, stating in no uncertain terms that any future misconduct would result in their arrest.

The second night passed off without incident but on the third night, whilst seeing the pubs out, I was confronted by the two again. I was subjected to calls of, "You are hiding behind your uniform," and further abuse which amused other pub goers spilling out of the nearby inns. I wasn't certain as to how long my posting to Wadebridge would last and most certainly was not looking forward to having to put up with this sort of abuse every time I was on night duty.

I had heard from one particular publican that these two

had been ruling the roost for a very long time but had never been taken to task by any of the constables.

By my last night of duty, I had had enough and told the two of them that if they wished to see me out of uniform, be at Wadebridge cattle market at eight p.m. the following evening.

The walk from my digs to the market only took five minutes and I really did wonder if they would turn up. They arrived by taxi, even though the pub they had been in was less than a quarter of a mile from the market. I could see that they had been drinking fairly heavily and I heard one of them telling the taxi driver to wait as what they had to do wouldn't take long. The first man, seeing me, charged rather foolishly with his arms flailing like a windmill, I sidestepped him and caught him a blow behind the ear, resulting in him going down and staying down. His mate tried to take advantage of the situation by trying a run, also with arms everywhere, but was no match for a sober man, therefore he joined his mate. I walked out of the market and home to bed. The taxi driver was still waiting.

The next morning whilst at breakfast I took a telephone call from the station sergeant to the effect that I was required at the police station immediately as the two men from the previous night were at the front of the station calling for me. I went straight to the station and sure enough, there they were. As soon as they saw me, they came towards me and I expected trouble. The elder of the two, before I could say anything, said, "We wanted to see you but the station door is locked – just to tell you, you are OK and if you need a hand with any trouble in the town…"

His mate then interjected with, "Or anyone sorting out, you can count on us."

I thanked them and then laid down the law, stating that I wanted no further trouble from them or any nonsense towards the other constables or public. They shook hands and went on their way. I was only stationed in Wadebridge for a year and during that time had no more trouble from either of them. In the old days, treating violence with violence had the necessary effect. I then, having watched the pair walk away, went into the police station. "What was all that about?" asked the sergeant.

"You don't want to know," was my reply.

Angela, my fellow lodger, and I had become very close and were, as stated in olden times, 'walking out'. The young baby boy who was living at the digs was quite a character. He had been placed there by his parents, who had split up. On one occasion when I was on traffic duty at the level crossing, I felt someone grab onto my legs from behind; it was the young boy, Michael. He had given his minder the slip and, having seen me, crossed the road. How he wasn't killed, I will never know – someone from above was looking after him that day.

Nothing fazed me much apart from one tour of night duty when I had a three a.m. point out in the countryside at a place called Bodieve. It was a pitch black winter's night and when I was still some quarter of a mile from my point, I was suddenly aware of a chain being dragged somewhere behind me. As I walked, the chain followed and when I stopped the chain stopped. I did this a couple of times – I stopped, the chain stopped. What made my mind begin to work overtime was that on this beat was a burial ground, and I felt the hair on my neck rise. My heart was thumping quicker. It reached a point where I was imagining all sorts of things and trying to reason out what I might find. I decided to walk backwards, draw my truncheon, and then switch on my torch to see what was following me. I started to walk and the chain started. I switched on my torch to see some twenty yards from me a large black and white collie dog with about fifteen feet of chain extending from his collar. I think the dog was as pleased to hear me talk to him as I was to see him. It turned out the dog had escaped from a farm and with a few enquiries the next day, it was returned to its owners.

As you have no doubt gathered, I had a bit of a reputation for not minding a bit of rough and tumble and for getting stuck in when the occasion arose, which brings me to the Great Train Robbery. I was on the evening shift and happened to be in the station in time to take a telephone call from the chief constable, which was a bit of a surprise. Apparently, a man called Bruce Reynolds had rung the headquarters information room stating that he was staying at a hotel in Port Isaac and believed the police were looking for him. The chief constable asked to be put through to the inspector's house and after a few minutes, the inspector arrived and I was sent back to my digs to put on civilian clothes as I was going to Port Isaac with the detective superintendent.

I crossed the bridge to await the arrival of the detective superintendent. After twenty minutes or so, he arrived accompanied by an inspector. I got into the back of the car and was handed a police gazette with a photo of one of the train robbers on it. The detective superintendent then spoke to me and informed me that the plan was that when we pulled into the hotel car park, I was to get out and enter the hotel, arrest the man – making sure he was not armed – and as soon as I had it under control, let him know and he would take over. I must have looked bemused as he then said, "I'm too near pension time to die." Which I believed, knowing the man, to be true.

I went into the hotel and asked to see the manager and explained the purpose of my visit. The manager looked embarrassed and explained that a group of friends were staying at the hotel, one of whom was called Reynolds and that after a few drinks and high spirits, Mr Reynolds had dialled 999 and said his piece – it was just a joke.

I said, "Some joke there, as the detective superintendent outside will not find this funny." I confirmed that Mr Reynolds was in the hotel.

"What do you suggest I do?" asked the manager.

I said, "I will go out and tell the superintendent and if he comes in, offer him a drink." As I walked out, I remember muttering to myself, 'he wouldn't lose his pension over this'.

The detective superintendent was not a happy man, but when I told him that Mr Reynolds was in the hotel and that the manager was going to provide drinks, his mood changed. The superintendent and inspector then went into the hotel and I went down to the village to get fish and chips. I hadn't had any tea.

I've already mentioned attending post-mortems and by now had attended several. On one occasion, I had to deal with the sudden death of an elderly lady who lived in a hamlet outside Wadebridge. It was normal for the hearse to call at the station to collect a constable for continuity in collecting the body to take it to the mortuary for the post-mortem. The hearse had a different driver to the normal one and he explained that it was his first time as the usual driver was sick.

We arrived at the cottage and as the deceased lady had no living relatives, I had the cottage door key, having been handed in by the nursing staff. As soon as I saw the lady, I realised there was no way we could get her downstairs in the coffin. One, because of her large size, and two, the twisting of the staircase. We had to lift the body from the bed onto a double blanket on the floor and manhandle her downstairs. I could see the hearse driver was unhappy with his role and, like me, was by this time was out of breath. We rested for a few moments and then with one last effort managed to lift the lady into the coffin.

Roger at Wadebridge, 1963

This was achieved but there was no way we could fasten the coffin lid as the lady was just too large. The only way was to get the coffin into the hearse and cover the top with a blanket. The cottage was fairly well hidden so there was no chance of anyone seeing what was taking place. I took the heavy end and the driver the feet end and we started to move round the side of the cottage. The next thing happened so quickly – the driver, who was walking backwards, stumbled and fell forward, wrenching the coffin from my hands, which, due to the way it fell, ended up with the lady partially covering the driver on the ground, who became very hysterical. I managed to retrieve the situation and we eventually got to the mortuary in one piece with me driving the hearse as the driver was not in a fit state.

Angela and I got married within the year and rented a small flat in Molesworth Street. I will always remember the black and white television set which worked off a TV aerial on a scaffold pole, which had to be twisted around each time we wanted to change channels.

Steam trains operated between Bodmin and Padstow, passing through the centre of Wadebridge where there was a signal box beside the level crossing gates over, what was then, the A39 main route. Once the crossing gates were closed, there would be quite a build-up of traffic each side. The constable on duty would have to remain at the junction to clear the traffic once the train had gone through. The daily signalman was called Jock, and he looked after whoever was on level crossing duty by making a cup of tea mid-morning, which we took in his signal box.

One morning, I received the thumbs up for tea and nipped smartly up to the signal box. No sooner had I done this, I noticed my inspector approaching the crossing. This was unprecedented, he never came out of his office until after lunch. I started to panic a bit as I couldn't see how to get out of the signal box without being seen, as I had no valid reason to be in there. Jock came up with the solution as only a signalman could. The train from Padstow was due any moment and as it approached he would hang out his bucket for coal from the signal box. As soon as the train stopped, I could climb from the signal box onto the footplate and travel the five hundred yards or so to the railway station and then walk down the road to the level crossing. It went to plan and as I approached the level crossing, the inspector was directing the traffic with his back to me. "Where have you been?" were his first words to me.

I replied, "Sorry, sir, I was took short with a tummy upset." Which, from the look on his face, seemed to satisfy him. I took over his position directing the traffic and he turned and walked away.

He stopped and said, "Just one thing, Harvey, it's about time you had clean gloves," and walked off. I had forgotten was to take off my white gloves off when climbing aboard the engine. The palm and fingers were black.

On another occasion, I was called to Bodmin police station to look after a fifteen-year-old boy who had beaten an old man to death in the grounds of St Laurence Hospital early one morning. The boy's mother came to the police station to see her son, accompanied by a priest, who started to talk to the boy about repentance. Without warning, the boy went berserk and I grabbed hold of him in order to restrain him and held him in a full nelson, at the same time suspending him from the ground but in his fury or mental condition, I could feel my fingers start to prise apart, such was his strength. I shouted at the priest, "For Christ's sake, get out." Which he did and immediately the boy calmed down. He was later detained at Her Majesty's pleasure.

I often smile at the thought of ordering a priest out for the sake of Christ.

There was a lot of pettiness in the force at times and on one occasion I was on duty on The Platt in Wadebridge dealing with a lady who had lost her handbag. I heard a car horn sounding and looked up from my writing to see a Triumph Herald on the opposite side of the road and a young man beckoning me to cross over to him. I ignored the driver until I had finished with the lady and then crossed the road. Seated beside the driver was a much older man who rather rudely asked me where the council offices were. I directed them to some two hundred yards away where the council offices were and the car drove off. Within twenty minutes of the car leaving me, the telephonist at the police station came running toward me, telling me to come back to the station immediately. I was met by the inspector, who informed me that the man in the passenger seat was the chairman of the Police Committee and I had failed to salute him. Furthermore, for this dereliction of duty, I was to catch the train to headquarters and appear in front of the assistant chief constable. This I did and was given a right dressing down. I later found out that the chairman had been to those council offices before. The driver of the car was a member of his own family to whom, I presume, he was trying to show how important he was.

CHAPTER 9

Angela and I, now being married, were termed as being on married strength and I received a married man's posting to the village of Stratton, further up the north Cornwall coast, a few miles from Bude.

Money was in short supply so Angela remained in her bank job in Wadebridge, lodging with friends. We did, however, manage to buy a secondhand minivan. At weekends I would fetch her on a Friday or Saturday and then drive her back to Wadebridge on a Monday, or if duty didn't permit, on the Sunday evening. It wasn't exactly the perfect arrangement for a newly married couple but it was the only way to save a bit.

The police station at Stratton was in the middle of the village and consisted of a central charge room with two cells and then on either side two police houses, one for the village constable and the other occupied by a motor patrol constable based in Bude. There were double front doors to the station which, when left open, led left into the guardroom and cells and the other into my sitting room, which when our furniture arrived and was being carried in, caused the whole floor of the sitting room to collapse. The police house had been unoccupied for some time and it took a couple of months before I could get it repaired.

Here I was in this large house, alone during the week with responsibility for quite a large farming area and a 250cc motorcycle to cover the area with. Across from the police station was the Bay Tree Hotel and I managed to have at least one hot meal a day there. The food was always good and reasonably priced.

The River Strat ran through the village and on my first day off I decided to follow it down through the valley. It was a lovely day and after about a mile I came to a field in which the hay was being turned by a farmer on a tractor. I leaned on the gate and watched. After a short while, the farmer drove over to the gate and asked if I was a holidaymaker as he hadn't seen me before. When I explained who I was, he invited me to his farmhouse where I met his wife. This was my introduction to the Wickett family of Marsh Farm.

Mrs Wickett's father had at one time been a police sergeant in Stratton, which was way before Bude had become an inspector's station. I should at this stage mention that the new inspector covering the Bude subdivision was Inspector Cole, who I had previously served under at Newquay. His uniform sergeant was Sergeant Thomas who, when at Newquay, was the detective sergeant.

The Wickett family consisted of Janet, their daughter and the eldest, twin boys, David and Philip, and a younger son called Keith, who I believe was about seven or eight years of age. I was made very welcome and I was happy to be back in the environment I loved. I was encouraged to ride the Wicketts' horses at every opportunity and in return helped out on the farm when off duty.

These were happy times with many amusing incidents. I remember in my second week in the village being called over by one of the oldest residents and told that one of my duties would be to put a fine set of antlers above the cottage door at the start of summer and to take them down before the onset of winter so they could be preserved.

I was cleaning my police motorcycle in front of the station one morning when a coach load of tourists stopped nearby. The driver came over to me and said they were a little early for their appointment in Bude and wondered if there was anything of interest in Stratton that his tourists could see. I pointed up the street a little way where my antler man was tending his garden. I explained that he was probably the man to ask as he had lived in the village all his life, whereas I was comparatively new to the area.

The coach driver went across to my antler man and after a few moments returned to the coach. "How did it go?" I asked.

"We're going up to the churchyard," he replied. "Apparently, everyone buried there are deaf and dumb."

They all moved off and I couldn't help walking over to the antler man and expressing my surprise that everyone in the churchyard was deaf and dumb.

He looked at me with a smile and said, "I thought you were smarter than that, because if you're dead you are bound to be deaf and dumb." A village character if ever there was one. I saw him trimming a piece of granite with a hammer and chisel one day and he was nearly ninety years old then.

Whilst at Newquay and Wadebridge, I had attended motorcar and motorcycle courses which qualified me for the traffic department should I be selected, but for the present time was happy with my country beat motorcycle.

In 1964 there was a gardening programme on TV presided over by a gent called Pop Welsh, and I was surprised one tea time to have a telephone call from him. Apparently, he had run a competition to find the longest runner bean in the south west and the winner was someone who lived in the countryside between Stratton and Holsworthy. The winner was not on the telephone but was required to be at the Plymouth studios to be filmed for the following week's show. Could I trace him from the details Pop Welsh had? If I could, a car would be sent to collect him and take him to the studio. I realised that the address was in the Devon force area but only a mile inside the border. I had a day off and thought I should help out, so I took the police motorcycle, set off and found the location. The cottage was like a picture from a chocolate box and the front garden was laid out with beautiful flowers with the back garden full of vegetables. The old gent and his wife were stunned by my news and agreed to visit the Plymouth studio the next day.

I returned home with a pannier full of runner beans, which were pressed on me by the happy couple. I rang Pop Welsh back and gave him the news.

The following week I tuned in to see Pop Welsh's gardening programme, during which the prize was presented to the man I had contacted. Pop Welsh turned to the camera and said, "I would like to thank PC Harvey of Stratton for making this presentation possible." A few minutes after the programme finished, the telephone rang. (You were always expected to answer the phone, even on your day off.) It was the inspector who, having watched the programme, wanted to know what part I had to play. When I told him, I was reminded that the hamlet I had visited was in the Devon force area. I mentioned that it was my day off when I delivered the message. Fortunately, the inspector didn't ask what mode of transport I had used.

Whilst at Stratton, I was sent on a CID course of instruction in Chelsea, London. Also present from Cornwall was Ivan Pollard and together we lodged at almost the end of the Bakerloo line, so it was quite a journey each way every day on the underground.

When I eventually returned to Stratton, I found that I was now allocated the traffic patrol motorcycle and was to act as relief driver on the patrol car but still covering anything on the Stratton beat.

Keith, the youngest of the Wickett farming family, often

talked about wanting to catch trout from the River Strat, which ran through his father's farm.

"How would you catch a trout?" he asked me one day.

I replied, "I would put a net across the river and then fifty yards further on put another across and see what happens."

He kept pestering me every time I saw the family and eventually agreed that the next day I would bring some net out. I laid the first piece of net then walked down the river to put the second piece out. It was then I noticed that Keith was missing. I looked around and saw him standing on the hedge looking up and down the road. I called out to him, asking what he was up to. He called back, "I'm keeping a look out for the police because we haven't got a license."

"Keith," I called back, "I am the police." We never did catch a fish.

Angela was now working in Bude, so it made life a lot easier. It was not permitted for police to do paid work outside of police duty but somebody thought I was working at Marsh Farm. In fact all I was doing was repaying the kindness of riding the farm's horses on my days off.

On one of my days off, I was cleaning out the stables on the farm when Mrs Wickett came down to the stable yard to say that a farmer on the other side of the valley had telephoned to say that there were two police officers in his field, apparently watching me through binoculars. I wasn't doing anything wrong and felt annoyed at this. I saddled one of the horses and, out of sight of the farm from where the call had come from, rode around the valley and came into the farm from a different direction. I saw the farmer, who pointed in the direction of where they were, quite close to an open gateway. I urged the horse, a big, seventeen hands hunter, into a canter then jumped the hedge. As I flashed over, I could see from the corner of my eye two startled figures following the appearance of the horse and rider. I carried on without stopping, down through the valley and back to the stables. A few days later, I was questioned by the inspector about where I was allowed to ride and had I seen anything suspicious at a certain farm? I pleaded ignorance, stating that I had permission to ride over all farmland in my area. I was asked if I received any payment for work of any type. I explained, most emphatically, what I did and that if anyone was complaining to come forward to be identified. That was the end of the matter.

The following week, I called at the farm from where the observations by the two policemen were kept, as a matter of courtesy to thank the farmer. He asked if I was in trouble and I answered, explaining my position. He started to laugh and said that he had found their car up the lane and stuffed a couple of potatoes up their exhaust pipe. Nothing was ever mentioned about this but one officer in particular could not look me straight in the eyes even when we met.

Just before finishing motorcycle patrol at midnight one evening, I did a trip through Bude and was surprised to see Brian Howells, a fellow country station constable of Whitstone village, kneeling beside his motorcycle in the main street. I stopped near him and he explained he had been called into Bude because of a staff shortage and was just starting off when the motorcycle chain had snapped. Although my machine was only equipped for a single rider, I offered to give him a lift home if he could manage to sit on my rolled up motorcycle coat. He would have to keep his feet off the twin exhaust pipes as they would get hot. We set off on the several miles to Whitstone and upon reaching the country station, Brian got off to find he had burnt through the soles of his Doc Martin boots by resting them on the exhaust pipes as his legs were tired.

One day whilst on motorcycle patrol and riding along the sea road at Widmouth, I was stopped by a family on holiday in the area, who were holding a young black and white collie dog which had no tail. Apparently, earlier, they had seen it thrown out of a car which had driven off but were so horrified by what they had seen they hadn't taken the registration number. They agreed to follow me home to Stratton police station where I took possession of the dog. As soon as I had finished duty, I took the dog to my friendly village vet. After a thorough examination, it was found to be in good health with no injury. The tail had been removed surgically some months previously. I knew exactly where the dog was going and that was Marsh Farm. Being a collie, he had the natural instinct to work both sheep and cattle. His only drawback being that on cornering he had no rudder to balance himself at speed and sometimes overshot himself. He was obviously named Bob Tail and lived for many years in a wonderful environment, being loved by all the family. From the time I took him to the farm to the time he died of old age, he would never ride in or on a vehicle. He had it in his mind that he was not going to be thrown from a moving vehicle again. A very wise boy.

CHAPTER 10

I recently attended the funeral of a retired police superintendent and as I sat in the chapel, I remembered an incident involving him during the three days of The Royal Cornwall Show at the Wadebridge show ground. I was on motorcycle patrol on the A39 north of the show site when I received a radio call to escort an ambulance from the Bodmin side of Wadebridge to the show ground, where a lady had been taken ill. I met the ambulance and commenced the escort, travelling at times on the opposite side of the road to clear the traffic. As I neared the destination, my route on the offside was clear apart from the superintendent standing in the middle of the offside lane. I had to swerve around him as he made no attempt to move. The ambulance followed me and disappeared into the show ground. I stopped and turned back to patrol, knowing that one of my colleagues would escort the ambulance to Truro City Hospital. As I rode back, I could see the superintendent still in the road and as I approached him he raised his hand to stop me, which I did. He said, "Do you realise you nearly killed me just now?" I was going to say something but he carried on: "You are suspended from riding, as from now." I still hadn't said anything and moved the motorcycle to a layby close by and parked it. I then started to walk towards the show ground.

The superintendent called to me, asking where I was going. I replied, "To try and find a lift home, sir."

He said, "Who's looking after the motorcycle?"

I said, "Not me, sir, I've been suspended."

He paused and then said, "Right, you take the motorcycle and this time I'll give you a caution. Understood?"

"Yes, sir."

The same superintendent once asked a probationary constable to give him 'in a nutshell' what he understood about the Larceny Act, which he did. The superintendent stated that the constable's answer was rather short. The constable then said, "You asked for it in a nutshell, sir."

"Yes," said the superintendent, "you gave it to me in a hazelnut, I wanted it in a coconut."

One the edge of the village was a small farm on which the farmer bred a few horses and also kept an old sow. The sow, left to her own devices most of the time, could often be seen on the main road. Members of the public would often report the sighting and I would notify the farmer.

Eventually, word of the wandering sow reached the inspector's office in Bude, after the sighting had been reported there by a holidaymaker. I was sent a memo by the inspector to see the farmer and report him for letting his animal stray on the highway

I arrived at the farm the next day in time to see the sow arriving back home again and reported the farmer for 'summons to court' for the offence, as instructed to do by the inspector.

The court day arrived and the farmer, represented by a well-known solicitor, pleaded not guilty.

In giving evidence, I was questioned by the solicitor, who asked, "Officer, which way was the sow going when you saw it?"

I replied, "Back to the farm, sir, where it had come from."

"So it was going home by itself?"

"Yes, sir."

The solicitor then addressed the magistrate. "I submit that if the sow was going home of its own volition, then it couldn't have been straying."

"Case dismissed."

I received a telephone call one evening from a man who wouldn't give his name but wanted to know what the law was as to shooting deer that wandered onto his land. I advised him against shooting the animals and explained the law.

"What if one got its antlers caught in a tree and couldn't

get free?"

I explained that in such a case it would be in order to shoot it.

"Perhaps you will now tell me your name," but the man hung up.

A week later, arriving back at the police station, I found a brown paper parcel on the station steps, attached to which was a note that read, 'This one had its antlers caught in a tree'. I didn't fancy it so I gave to my 'antler man', who later informed me it was the best bit of venison he had ever tasted.

By now Inspector Cole had departed and a newly promoted one arrived at Bude; his first task was to remonstrate with one of the constables who he had seen whilst on duty having his hair cut.

When asked for an explanation, the constable replied, "Well, it grows on duty time so I thought it was correct to have it cut in duty time, sir."

One winter's evening, on the four till midnight patrol, I called at the Wicketts' farm for a cup of tea, having missed my meal break through having to deal with an accident. I parked near the farmhouse back door so that I could hear the police radio. The twin boys, Phillip and David, were somewhere down in the collecting yards. After about ten minutes, I had a radio call to attend an accident in Bude main street. I left the farmhouse kitchen and into the yard which was completely dark and I had to grope along the wall to reach my machine. The yard light was on when I rode up so I thought the bulb must have fused. I got on the machine, kicked it into life and set off towards Bude. As I entered Bude town, which was well lit, I noticed a group of people outside the first pub, who pointed at me and waved. I acknowledged them and rode on. I soon arrived at the scene of the accident (which fortunately, was non-injury), brought my machine to a halt, flicked out my side stand and got off. To my horror I saw on the aerial on the back of the motorcycle about twenty apples like an upright row of conkers. The twins had struck and turned off the yard light, hoping I wouldn't notice what they had done. I explained to those involved in the accident what had happened and everyone had a good laugh. The apples were OK apart from a hole in each and one of the ladies involved in the accident took them to make apple pie. I was the first traffic officer to supply fruit at an accident.

Life was fairly normal until one morning when the postman called at the station to inform me he had been on his rounds on the council estate at the top end of Stratton and found one of the residents slouched on his doorstep crying. The postman felt something was very wrong and therefore decided to let me know.

I rode straight up to the estate and from what the postman had told me, easily found the address. The man was still sitting on his doorstep, wiping his eyes. I enquired what the problem was and he told me his wife was in the house having committed suicide. The postman must have notified the cottage hospital as well, because at that moment Doctor Blood (that was his real name), the village doctor arrived.

We entered the house and in the kitchen was a lady sitting on a chair with her head resting on the cooker. There were lots of empty pill containers lying around. A smell of burning flesh had filled the air and I then saw a cigarette between her fingers, still very much alight.

Doctor Blood made a quick examination of the lady and confirmed that she was still alive. An ambulance was sent for and arrived, taking the lady off to Plymouth Hospital.

Doctor Blood and I talked for a few minutes and then started to walk towards the front door when he turned and asked me if I had seen any blood on the lady. I told him I hadn't seen any. He pointed to the lino covering the stairs leading up from the hallway and said, "That looks like blood." On closer examination, blood could be seen on each step. I carefully went up the stairs trying to keep clear of the bloody footprints and on reaching the landing, saw the body of a young woman lying in a pool of blood with her skull smashed in. Close by was an axe. Through the bathroom door, I could see the bath was half full of water and bits of skull and hair on the taps. The water was bloody and it looked as if the body had been dragged from the bathroom onto the landing and then assaulted again with the axe. Doctor Blood confirmed death and I got hold of the inspector at Bude.

A patrol car was despatched to try to catch up with the ambulance because of the possible murder connection.

I was instructed to stay in the council house until the detective superintendent arrived. Another constable was stationed outside in the garden.

The man who had been crying was now being looked after by a neighbour. I had been in the house for nearly an hour when suddenly the bathroom bath tap came on full bore with a rushing sound. I completely froze and my heart was pounding, at the same time thinking that the young woman had got up and was washing herself in the bathroom. I then reasoned that this was not possible and went up the stairs, stepping over the body, and turned the tap off. Unfortunately, it was the tap with the most skull and bloody hair on it. The theory later put forward was that there must have been an airlock in the system which eventually gave way to the pressure built up in the tank.

It was also established that the young lady was the daughter of the lady taken to Plymouth in the ambulance. It appeared that mother and daughter had an argument the previous evening. The father had gone to work as a baker in the early hours, after which it seems that mother and daughter started rowing again and the mother killed the daughter. The father it appears, didn't know his daughter was lying dead in the house.

The ambulance reached Plymouth but the lady had died. A very sad episode for all concerned.

One evening whilst on patrol, I was sent to investigate a fight at a pub in Marhamchurch, a small village a few miles from Bude. I set off, crossed the A39 and started down the narrow road leading to the village. It was dark and close to eleven p.m. as I approached a bend and dip in the road, which was only a car's width. I was suddenly confronted with a car immediately coming towards me with no lights on. I couldn't avoid it as there wasn't enough room to go either side and ended up striking it head on. The force of the collision, fortunately for me, having let go of my handle bars, threw me up into the hedge and my clothing saved me from injury. My motorcycle was embedded in the front of the car but I managed to open a pannier and get out my torch. I went to the driver's side of the car and tapped on the window. The car lights were still off and I tapped on the window again and this time it was slowly wound down. I shone the torch on myself to be identified and saw a man accompanied by a woman. The man, on seeing me, said in an inebriated voice, "A policeman. How did you get here so quick?"

Unfortunately this wasn't the only accident I was personally involved in. I couldn't get radio reception in Stratton village and had to climb out of the valley for about a mile in order to book on or off, I was travelling uphill at about midnight when a farm dog came out of a field gate and collided with my front wheel. The bike went over, fortunately this time without damage but the kick start and foot rest broke the tibia and fibula in my right leg above the ankle and below the knee. I was rescued soon afterwards and taken to Plymouth Hospital where my leg was plated, but due to complications I had to stay in hospital for a few weeks.

In the large ward was a young man who scooted around in a wheelchair. He was apparently a bit of a tearaway and had numerous motorcycle accidents and been to court a few times. He let it be known he hated coppers but as time went on curiosity got the better of him when he knew I was a motorcycle patrol constable. He came to my bedside after lunch one day and told me he had eaten eighteen roast potatoes and was still feeling hungry. I kept a straight face and said, "You've probably got a tape worm."

He said, "What's that?"

"It's a large snake-like worm that lives in your stomach and gobbles up everything you eat. That's why you are always hungry."

"Are you sure?"

"Yes."

The next morning was the surgeon's round of the ward and precisely at eleven, Mr Lilly, the surgeon, accompanied by the matron and junior doctors, entered the ward and started on the opposite side of the ward from me talking to each bed-ridden patient. After some fifteen minutes or so, the party reached Allen's bed. The ward in those days, on the surgeon's round, was always quiet.

Mr Lilly asked, "How are you today, Allen?"

"Not so good."

"Why is that?"

"I've got a large tapeworm."

"What?"

"And I want to know what you are going to do about it."

Hearing this, all I wanted to do was disappear but could

only wonder what was coming next.

"Who told you about the tapeworm?"

"That copper over there," Allen said, pointing at me.

"It's OK, I'll sort the tapeworm out for you so don't worry."

After a further fifteen minutes, the surgeon and his followers arrived at my bedside. Mr Lilly looked me in the eye and said, "I think you had better stick to the law and leave me to do the doctoring."

On my release from hospital, I was told by Mr Lilly to forget motorcycles and horses for a while as he wasn't sure I would get full movement in my ankle joint. Having always been active and a bit strong-headed, within a week of getting the plaster off I was in the saddle of one of the quieter horses and the exercise helped me get one hundred percent movement back. The surgeon was surprised when I saw him and I was soon riding the motorcycle again.

Whilst on patrol through the village one morning, I was stopped by one of the residents who showed me his front garden where someone had cut and taken his beautiful show of Arum Lilies. Footprints in the earth looked like a couple of small people were responsible. No one had apparently seen anything relating to the theft, which remained a complete mystery until a few days later when, in conversation with the vicar, I was informed that a large bunch of Arum Lilies had appeared on the altar having been donated by two young boys from the village. The gentleman from whose garden they were taken was most forgiving and requested no further action be taken.

On one of my days off, I went out to Marsh Farm to assist with the corn harvest. An agricultural contractor who lived in Stratton village arrived at the farm with his combine harvester, which was one of the early models. The driver sat at the front, which was cabless, and the reaped corn was collected at the side in hessian bags from the corn holding tank. The bags, as they were filled, were then tied and placed in line on a chute which could be off-loaded at any point in the field. I was filling the bags and young Keith, who was home from school, was tying them. Things were going well in the twenty acre corn field until it came to reaping a very steep section. As we reached the steepest part, the combine came to a halt as the large centre drive wheel started to dig itself into the soil. The driver called back to us to hold onto the guardrail as he was going to try and reverse. This he did successfully but instead of stopping the machine, started to move backwards and to gather speed. The driver shouted, "No brakes." I grabbed hold of Keith and leapt over the guardrail landing on the soft soil as the combine sped past us

To my utter amazement, the driver stayed with the combine and all I could do was watch, expecting the machine to crash into the hedge and disintegrate. The driver had other ideas and as he reached the hedge at the bottom of the field, he pulled hard on the steering wheel, the effect was to turn the whole machine at an angle so that it partially mounted the hedge and stopped.

The engine was still going and then, to my complete astonishment, the driver took out his pipe, lit it and commenced to drive up the field to us. When he reached us, his only comment was, "OK, boys, we're ready to roll again." The field was finished without further incident and if ever a man deserved an award for coolness, it was him.

On another occasion, I was on motorcycle patrol and riding from Stratton through the back lanes to Marhamchurch, when I came across the twin boys, David and Philip. They had a tractor and trailer stuck in the lane ditch. It transpired that they had driven out of the field without waiting for their father and took too tight a turn, hence the ditch. Philip asked me to sit on the tractor seat as their father would be arriving in a couple of minutes

"Why me?" I enquired.

"He won't say anything to you but we will be in for it for moving the tractor," said David.

I declined to help with a smile and said they would have to suffer the consequences this time.

I was cleaning the police motorcycle at the front of the station one morning. The weather was beautiful, in spite of the overnight rain, and I could hear the sound of an old tractor approaching from the far side of the village. I was aware of the tractor passing over the bridge and then coming to a halt a few feet from me. I glanced up and froze in horror at what I saw. The driver was a local farmer and at the rear of his tractor was a small flatbed trailer, upon which lay the body of what looked like a farm worker. I glanced at the farmer for an explanation and my look prompted him to say, "This is old Bill who worked for me. He died up in the field this morning."

I said, "Has he been seen by a doctor?"

"No. I could see he was dead and the field is full of mud so I thought I had better bring him down."

I dropped everything and ran into the police station and fetched a blanket from the cell and covered the poor fellow up.

The station was only about five hundred yards from the cottage hospital so I got the farmer to drive to it and from where the man was pronounced dead. I was glad of a strong cup of tea after the event.

On one Christmas day lunchtime, I answered a ring on the station door to find a middle-aged man in a state of agitation. He informed me that his wife had threatened him with a knife and chased him around the bedroom. I reminded him what day it was and that he should make peace with his wife and therefore should go home. This he did, but within the hour he was back ringing the doorbell again, saying the same thing was happening again and he didn't want to go home. I was a bit cheesed off by now and advised him that the only thing I could do was let him sit in the cell until he decided what he was going to do. He readily agreed to this.

I checked on him a couple of times that afternoon and could see he was fast asleep. It was now seven p.m. and I was trying to decide what the best plan would be when the station doorbell rang. Standing on the steps was a woman with two young children hanging on to her coat. She immediately apologised for disturbing me on Christmas Day but was concerned for the safety of her husband, who had left home at lunchtime and not returned. I invited her into the station charge room and then to follow me to the cells where lay Sleeeping Beauty. I asked if she recognised the man and she of course immediately confirmed it was her missing husband. By now the man was awake and on seeing his family burst into tears. I invited them to sit around the charge room table and not row, but wait till I returned.

Angela had put together some refreshments for the family and differences were soon sorted out with a bit of advice from me.

They left the station and during the rest of my stay at Stratton I heard no more from them.

A new bungalow had been built at Marsh Farm for Mr and Mrs Wickett, with a balcony from which steps led down to the garden. They had moved into the bungalow with all new furnishings and, in the lounge, a beautiful three piece suite. It was a lovely summer's day and Mrs Wickett had opened the French windows to let some air in. The farm's sheepdogs lived in kennels near the cowsheds, apart from a very old terrier called Tina that lived in the farmhouse in a basket close to the Aga. The two sheepdogs normally ran behind the tractor on the way back from the fields after checking the sheep and then waited in the cattle yard to be kennelled once their duty was done. Mr Wickett was quite puzzled as after parking the tractor he couldn't see the dogs and despite whistling and shouting nothing happened. A short distance from the farm building ran the stream so he assumed the dogs had gone for a wallow in the water. After some half hour passed there was still no sign of the dogs and it was then that he heard Mrs Wickett calling with a sense of urgency in her voice. He ran up to the bungalow to find the two sheepdogs had been playing in the stream, and then led by Tina, the terrier, had entered the lounge via the front garden and balcony where they were now stretched out on the three piece suite. Everyone thought it was funny apart from Mrs Wickett.

Chapter 11

It was now 1967 and we were amalgamating with Devon, Exeter and Plymouth constabularies. The old assistant chief constable had retired and Mr Pill, who had taken over from Mr Keast at Penzance when I was there, was now the new district commander in charge of Cornwall. I was surprised one day to receive a personal call from him, asking if I would like a posting to Truro as a detective constable. I readily accepted the posting although I knew I would miss the country life.

Having been allocated a police house in Truro, we moved and I met the Criminal Investigation Department staff at Truro. The detective inspector was Ginger Williams, who was a detective constable at Penzance when I was a cadet. John 'Chippy' Chapman, the detective sergeant, Roger Jacob, Ivan Pollard and Les Pearce, whose place I was taking on his impending move to Newquay on promotion to detective sergeant. Ivan and I had been together on the London Criminal Investigation Department course.

I was missing the horse side of my life, especially the riding exercise, but as luck would have it I had to assist the Probus village constable on a burglary investigation one day and in passing conversation mentioned something about horses. He mentioned he had a farmer with several horses on his patch and when he was that way, he would call in for me. Within a couple of days, I had a call from the farmer, a Mr Roberts, asking me to call and see him, which I did. He kept three show jumpers and was a top man in the south western jumping scene. I was given a test ride and from there on would ride on my days off and sometimes early in the morning before work.

I believe the horses to be the fittest I have ever ridden and you were kept on your toes all the time you were in the saddle, but nevertheless, extremely enjoyable.

I was on call one night when the telephone rang at about two a.m. It was the uniform duty sergeant, who informed me that he and his night crew had arrested five young men seen running away from the Moorfield car park in the city centre. A number of petrol cans, partly filled, and a syphoning kit had been beside cars in the car park. There had been a spate of petrol thefts from around the city for some time, so this was a good result. I got dressed and drove to the station to assist with the interviews as requested, but to my annoyance, when I arrived, I found that all five were sitting together in one room. I soon realised that was why I had been called, they were not admitting anything. The uniform sergeant should have split them up on arrest, so now they had had a chance to get their stories straight. I spoke to all five together, "I understand you have nothing to do with the petrol thefts, even though you were seen running away from the car park."

"That's right," said one of the five, who I presumed to be the leader as he was very cocky.

I said, "In that case, I am going to carry out an experiment. What I intend to do is to light my lighter and ask all five of you to open your mouths. If you haven't syphoned petrol this night, then you are free to leave. If, however, you have syphoned petrol, as I walk past with my lighter, it will blow your bloody heads off."

I took my lighter out and lit it, then walked towards the first chap who rather hastily said, "There's no need for that, I did some of the syphoning." I looked at the others who were nodding in agreement with the first chap. Fingerprints were subsequently found on the cans and previous thefts were also admitted.

Angela and I had been trying for a family for several years without success and to make matters worse, her younger brother's wife gave birth to a baby girl. We were asked to be godparents. I consulted our doctor, who advised and arranged for me to have a test, and, if all proved OK with me, then Angela could have one. I eventually had an appointment at the City Hospital. At the hospital, I had a bottle thrust into my hand and a toilet door pointed out where I had to go to produce a sample.

Later that day, when Angela arrived home from her bank job, she asked me how I had got on at the hospital.

I explained that it was quite an experience and she said, "What happened?"

"At the hospital, they have a special suite, beautifully furnished with a king size water bed. I was taken to the room by one of the nurses and told to take a shower, after which, I should lay on the bed naked."

"What then?" she said.

"Soft music started to be piped to the room and the curtains on one side opened and this beautiful nurse entered and started to undress."

"No, really?"

"Yes, and, of course, I was aroused immediately and the nurse placed a condom on me and we made love for several minutes, after which she took the sample away for testing."

"I can't believe it. Are you telling the truth?"

"Yes and believe it or not I have to go back tomorrow and do it all again in case the first sample is inconclusive."

I started to laugh and then she realised the leg pull and I had to tell the truth.

The result came through and I was found to be the problem.

The doctor advised that nothing could be done other than after intercourse to suspend my wife's legs in the air from the ceiling for an hour to give the sperm a chance to complete their journey. Naturally, Angela didn't fancy that. I felt we didn't get married just to have children but I could see that she desperately wanted a family, and sadly we eventually divorced. Angela went on to marry and have a daughter of her own, which made me pleased for her.

Truro police station was a very old building on the edge of the city and everyone worked out of small, cramped offices. A short distance from the police station were the Automobile Association offices, and the first floor was up for rent. It was an ideal opportunity, so the divisional staff moved out and into the new Automobile Association building. Before this came about, and to actually see the cramped conditions we were working in, the county surveyor and headquarters staff were to inspect the old building. Along the corridor from the CID office was a ladies' toilet facing the corridor and as the group came along on their tour of inspection, they found Chippy sitting on the toilet with a typewriter on his lap. It was taken in good heart and everyone had a good laugh.

We took over the old admin office which was twice the size we were used to. The divisional staff were now settled in the Automobile Association building a short distance away.

We had a new staff member arrive called Brian Blake. Inspector Williams was gone and my old inspector from Newquay, Mr Osborne, arrived as our CID chief. Next door to the new CID office, was a toilet with a washbasin, which was handy for filling the kettle. One morning, a hastily arranged conference was held in our office, which the detective chief superintent and deputy were to attend.

Chippy offered to make tea or coffee, which everyone accepted. Chippy went into the toilet, filled the kettle and then flushed the toilet and came back into the CID room pretending to wipe the kettle with his handkerchief. I knew what he was up to and I could see the strange looks on the officers' faces, as they thought he had filled the kettle from the toilet. We drank our coffee but it was noticeable that the officers left theirs.

I remember an occasion when we arrested an eighty-five-year-old shoplifter. Chippy came into the interview room looking very serious and said to the old gent, "Now, before we start this interview, I want to know if your mother and father know you are out on your own?" The old gent was cautioned and taken home.

Ivan had by now been promoted and left our office. I had been promoted to detective sergeant and stayed in the department and Detective Constable George Tippet arrived.

Everyone got on well and we had a good detection rate. Brian was a scruffy dresser in no uncertain terms. One winter's morning he came to work with open-toed sandals, a red shirt, blue trousers and a white, ship's captain type jacket with a large brown stain on its sleeve, which Brian maintained had been left by the ship's captain's parrot.

This particular morning, George, who had a very pock-marked face, couldn't help himself. He looked at Brian and said, "Here he comes, Tancock's bloody fair," and added, "God, it is Easter already."

Brian, quick as a flash retorted, "That's OK, George, it's

better than having a face like a half-bitten Aero bar."

George was out of his chair and grabbed hold of Brian, but my size and rank cooled the tempers.

A lot of CID work came in over the telephone or by personal callers to the guardroom, which was always open to the public. I was asked to see a local businessman and his wife one morning when they called at the station very upset.

Their story was that they had three sons. The two eldest were working in their business but the youngest, aged eighteen, had gone off the rails, left his schooling and had now taken over their house and kicked them out. The other brothers were afraid of him and the parents were staying in a hotel where they had been for the last few days. The young son had changed the locks and barricaded himself into the large detached house. Friends had been to the house but he refused to open the door or to speak to anyone. Having listened to their story, I asked if any deliveries were to be made to the house. The husband said, "We bought a new television from Currys but we have put it on hold for the moment."

I asked if there was a TV in the house and was told yes but it was on the blink, hence the new one on order.

I asked them to leave it with me and I would contact them later. I went to Currys. I knew the manager and asked to borrow one of their blue coats with Currys printed on it. I then asked for an empty television box.

I got one of the lads to drive me to the house but he was to remain out of sight until I called.

I walked up the drive and to the front door, dressed as

Mr Curry, carrying my TV box. I rang the doorbell and after a short while, a face appeared at the letterbox and said, "What do you want?"

I said, "I've got the new TV to be installed."

"Leave it on the doorstep."

"I can't do that, it has to be set up and I'm to take the old one away and I need your signature."

There was a pause and then the door opened. I said, "Can you give me a hand, this box is heavy."

He said, "OK."

As he leaned forward to take his side of the box, I dropped it. The last thing he knew was when he hit the floor and I was putting a pair of bracelets on him. The mother and father were soon back in their home and the son appeared in court where he learned his lesson. A few weeks later, the mother and father called at the police station with a rather nice gift of a photo album, duly endorsed by them for me.

I had now met Rossanah and we had become an item. I had explained to her that it was unlikely that I could have children. She told me that it wasn't a problem as she didn't want children.

Geoff Gedge, a new detective constable, had arrived and worked well into our team.

Kidnapping is quite a rare offence, so it came as a surprise when a message was circulated throughout the force area to the effect that a lady and young daughter had been taken by force from the London area and were now believed to be in the Looe area of Cornwall.

A couple of days later, we received a message from Liskeard CID to the effect that a note had been recovered from a ladies' toilet in Liskeard, which had seemingly come from the lady, to the effect they were making their way to Falmouth. The car make and registration were also included. It was a question of moving very quickly and I got hold of a dog handler who had his own car to follow me to a place called Truck Fork, near Probus, where the car would most certainly come if on the way to Falmouth (the Probus bypass hadn't been built then). Truck Fork was a good place to ambush the car. I didn't want to use a traffic car in case the man panicked, as it was unknown whether he was armed. I was in my blue Mini when I saw the car coming towards Truck Fork and simultaneously the dog handler and I converged on the car, forcing it to stop. I quickly jumped out, opened the car door and grabbed hold of the driver and hauled him out. The dog handler then took over and conveyed the man to Truro police station.

The woman, who was in the back of the car with her daughter, burst into tears and I ended up taking her to Truro Hospital for trauma treatment.

The man had apparently rented a holiday cottage near Looe, kidnapped the woman and child and sexually abused the woman for over a week. He had driven to Liskeard for food when she asked to go to the toilet, hence the note.

Having seen the state of the woman, it made me realise that for some people, heaven and hell are all around us.

As I have touched on religion, I recall a story about my cousin, a chaplain in the navy. He was on a Destroyer one day in the Mediterranean and had to be taken off and put back on an aircraft carrier. He was to be taken off by helicopter and put into a harness. What he didn't know was that the helicopter pilot had made a secret arrangement with the captain of the aircraft carrier. It was a warm day and the Mediterranean was flat calm and, as the helicopter neared the carrier, the crew lowered Cousin David down to within a few feet of the sea. David thought something had gone wrong with the lifting gear and of course started to panic, waving his legs about. The captain of the aircraft carrier announced over the tannoy for all the crew to report to port side and watch the chaplain walking on water.

From time to time, we have probationary constables attached to the department for a month's training and one chap in particular would, when we had morning coffee, wait until everyone had heads down and working, put his hand in his coat pocket and sneak out a biscuit without anyone noticing – so he thought. One morning he went through the same procedure, when suddenly Brian looked up and said, "I've been wondering if you can peel an orange in your pocket as well without us knowing." It was then that everyone burst into laughter.

Across the road from the police station was a row of cottages and in one lived an odd family. One evening, the eldest daughter of the family came running into the police station shouting that her father was drunk and had put his head in the oven to commit suicide. A couple of uniform staff ran across the road to try and save the man, only to find him lying on the floor with his head inside the electric oven!

I had a visit one day from two bank inspectors who asked me to take on a case connected to the bank involving one of their managers. The manager had been interviewed and suspended from work and the bank thought the police should follow it up with a prosecution.

In examining all the paperwork, I found what the manager had done was to call in about twenty of his best clients, who had business interests, and offer them overdrafts at seven percent and then tell them that he would re-invest their overdraft facility with a private company for thirteen percent with a promise that over a period of time, their overdrafts would be cleared and leave them with a nice profit. Although the manager had got away with it for quite some time and had used the clients' overdrafts for his own purposes, i.e., holidays, golf and the night life. It was picked up by the bank's inspectors who didn't get an admission from him.

I took statements from the client list, given to me by the bank, over the next couple of weeks and then on a Sunday morning called at the bank manager's house. He was still in bed when I arrived and he eventually presented himself. He was most reasonable and wanted to talk about everything other than the crime. He tried to ring his solicitor but was unable to reach him. As it was now approaching lunchtime, his wife appeared with a snack for us. I then indicated that perhaps the interview would be best conducted at Truro police station. He said, "If I tell the exact truth, will I be arrested?"

I said, "Providing I'm satisfied, I can arrange for you to be dealt with by way of summons." I then related details of the witness statements, which he admitted.

The manager eventually appeared in court and was given a custodial sentence. He came over as a really nice person, very intelligent and I couldn't understand how he didn't expect to be found out. The bank, at the end of the trial, paid all the clients that were involved, the difference between what the overdraft was and what had been promised. They all did very well and had nothing but praise for their former manager.

Situated in a small hamlet just outside Truro lived a petty criminal who had a large family by his first wife and several children by his second wife. He also had a large drink problem and at times disappeared for days on end.

I knew then that when he was very drunk or away his wife was sleeping with another convicted criminal who was also involved in the criminal world with the husband.

I took a call one morning from the South Wales police, to the effect that a man identified from fingerprints had been taken on by a south west haulage firm as a driver and on his first trip had disappeared with a load of tins of meat, fruit and several hundredweight of Kerry Gold butter and the driver had been identified as our man. Later that day I visited his home and was informed by his wife that she didn't know where he was and hadn't heard from him for over a week. The wife was a lot younger than her husband, quite attractive and was never rude or aggressive when questioned and always turned her six children out well, in spite of her husband's behaviour.

The following day, I had another call from the South Wales police, stating that the missing lorry had turned up burnt out near a gypsy camp in Cornwall. Enquiries revealed that the contents of the lorry, apart from the butter, had been used in the camp site for a family wedding. There was still no sign of the missing driver.

Later that evening, I took a call from a petty criminal asking if I was looking for Kerry Gold butter. The caller needed some money, so I arranged to meet and he handed me a pack of Kerry Gold (at that time Kerry Gold was not sold in West Country shops). As a result of what he told me, I went to a local inn and persuaded the landlord to let me look in his pub kitchen, and there I discovered, in freezers and cabinets, some four hundredweight of Kerry Gold butter. With a bit of persuasion, I got the landlord to say where he had obtained it and, lo and behold, it had been sold to him by the missing driver's wife's lover. He had also sold butter to another inn where his wife worked. This man was working locally and I managed to find him. He admitted to selling the butter very cheaply and also that he knew it was probably stolen in view of from who he had obtained it. Having kept in contact with the South Wales police, I charged him and then released him on bail. At lunchtime the next day, I took a call from an unknown male who informed me that the man I was looking for was now at home.

In the 1960s, each CID officer used his own car for

police work and mine, at that time, was a blue Mini and it was not at all unusual for each CID member to work a case on his own unless there was more than one to arrest.

I once again drove out to where the man lived, parked my car and walked up the path to his house, and through the glass front door I could see him in the sitting room slouched in a chair watching television, with empty beer cans on the floor around the chair. I knocked on the door, which he chose to ignore, and then I knocked louder, to which he shouted, "Come in." I entered; he knew who I was from previous encounters. He didn't switch the TV off so I questioned him over the volume. He didn't take his eyes off the screen and ignored me. I decided at that moment to arrest him and informed him; he wasn't a very big man but was known to be aggressive at times. As I finished my speech, he suddenly threw his beer can across the room and then grabbed hold of a hammer that I hadn't seen but had been somewhere at the side of his chair. He hurled it at the TV, which, on impact, exploded.

The seatbelt laws had not come into force but manufacturers had put anchorage points in most vehicles and after the hammer throwing, I grabbed hold of the man, handcuffed him and placed him on the rear seat of my Mini, his hands in front of him on the floor, securely fastened to the seatbelt anchorage point. I had no more nonsense on the way to the police station, where he was detained. Later that evening, I took a call from the man who had distributed the butter to the two pubs, asking if the man in custody was being kept in or being released. I informed him that he was to remain in custody and asked him, "Why the concern?" He said he was ringing on behalf of the man's wife. My mind was telling me a different story so, as the man in custody had, as we say, cleaned his sheet having admitted the theft of the lorry and contents, I decided to bail him and as it was now late in the evening, drove him to his house. He got out of the car and walked up the path. I stood at the bottom of the path and watched. After a few minutes a bedroom light came on and I could hear a lot of shouting and the silhouettes of two men fighting. I got in my car and drove off. I had witnessed the end of a beautiful friendship between two hardened criminals.

Brian was the joker in the office and took great delight in creating havoc at times. One particular day, I had spent most of my time typing a complicated naturalisation report, as the CID typist was off sick, and as it neared six o'clock, I had managed to complete the last page of the report, which I left in the typewriter whilst I went to get a drink from the kitchen. On my return to the office, I went to take the typing from the typewriter when, to my horror, I saw typed in red ink at the bottom of the report, 'Please retype this again'. Brian had struck again and I was fuming. A few minutes later, Brian returned to the office with Roger Jacob, who I instructed to lock the CID office door. I then grabbed hold of Brian, pinned him down and stripped all his clothes off him and dropped them out of the window onto the street below. Roger J and I then left the office and parked up the road but in sight of the clothes. I had instructed the duty constable in the public office not to give him any assistance whatsoever.

A few minutes later, we saw a figure come out of the police station wrapped in a sheet of brown paper, through which a hand extended to pick up the clothes.

Brian had been paid back in full.

At the entrance to Truro Magistrates Court was a ladies' hat shop, run by a delightful lady called Mrs Preedy who, like most of us, enjoyed a lunch snack in Roger Scott's nearby pub. Several solicitors from city offices also took refreshment there. We got to know Mrs Preedy quite well and one lunchtime. She ordered her normal sausage, which was placed on the counter by Roger Scott. As she turned away to speak to someone, Chippy reached out, took that sausage and ate it. What followed was chaos as Mrs Preedy alarmed the whole pub by her loud accusations but we did pay for another sausage soon after.

A few weeks later, when entering the court, Mrs Preedy accosted me with a large catalogue in her hands and said, "I know your secret."

"What secret?"

"Your part-time job."

"I don't know what you are talking about."

She then pointed to a photograph in the catalogue, which was of a man modelling pyjamas and who could have been my double, but obviously wasn't me. I decided to have a bit of a game and begged her not to tell anybody about my modelling work. For several years after, Mrs Preedy, who believed I was the man in the catalogue would say when we happened to meet, "Your secret is still safe with me."

I had a telephone call one day from the lady proprietor of a horse retail business. She wanted to speak to me as she was concerned about some people who had tried to sell her a falabella, which is a pony of about thirty inches in height and expensive. As a result of what she said, a search was made of a property in the town of Penryn where, in the back yard, tied up to a tap, was a falabella. The people who lived in the property could not give a satisfactory explanation as to ownership, stating that the pony had been brought down from Yorkshire in the back of a caravan by two men. I made arrangements for the pony to be moved to a stable yard at nearby Mylor for safe keeping. The following week a piece about the pony was put in the local newspaper.

That week a retired police officer from Yorkshire was on holiday in Falmouth and in a local barber's waiting for a haircut and reading the local paper, when to his amazement read about the pony which in fact belonged to his daughter. It had been stolen from the yard where it was kept by none other than the two men who had brought it to Cornwall, one of whom had connections with the livery yard from which it was stolen. Having returned to Yorkshire, they were traced and charged with the theft.

One evening whilst on duty, I heard over the radio about two ponies that had escaped from their paddock on the outskirts of the city and had run into the car park of the

Brookfield Hotel, about five hundred yards from the police station. I went up to the hotel and could see the ponies at the top of the car park. Several people were now on the scene, including the owners of the ponies. Leading off the car park to a sunken area was the roof of the staff quarters, the roof being some four feet above the car park level. I urged everyone not to make a noise and just let the ponies settle. It worked very well and one of the ponies came towards us and was caught. Just then the lights of a car swung into the far side of the car park onto the other pony, which startled it so much that it leapt up onto the staff quarters roof. Unfortunately, the roof was made of asbestos sheeting and the weight of the pony caused it to collapse and the pony disappeared into the void. I rushed round to the front of the living quarters, opened the bedroom door, expecting to see either a dead or badly injured pony, only to see it standing four square on the bed where it had landed. It was completely still and I put a head collar on it and walked it calmly off the bed and out to the car park. A quick check revealed no injury, which was a miracle.

A report came in one day from a distraught lady to the effect that her cob type horse had been stolen from her field some six miles outside Truro. She suspected a dealer who tried to buy the horse from her and to whom she had refused to sell it.

The dealer, a local man, was seen but denied all knowledge. A description of the horse was circulated.

It was August and the weather was very warm, when a

few days after the theft had been reported, a lady called at the police station asking if the police could get hold of the RSPCA as there was a horse in a field behind County Hall with its head covered in hundreds of flies. Because of my interest in animals, I was informed and agreed to take a look. As soon as I reached the field gate, where the horse was standing, I could see what the lady meant. The horse's head was literally covered in hundreds of flies. Normally you would get a few in the summer but not this amount. I had a head collar and lead rope in my car and went into the field. The horse was good as gold as I put the head collar on it. Then I swatted the flies and ran my hand down the face of the horse, only to find that the whole of its white face had been covered in Marmite, obviously to disguise it. This was the stolen horse.

Enquiries revealed that the field in which the horse was found had been rented by our suspect, the dealer, a few weeks before the theft. He was arrested and sentenced for this offence.

One evening, Chippy and I were getting ready to leave the CID office when we heard a commotion from the floor below. We left the office very quickly and started to descend the stairs when we were confronted by one of our well-known criminals who had a history of violence. On the floor at the bottom of the stairs was the duty uniform sergeant who was just getting to his feet, having been floored by this particular individual. They say that great minds think alike and in an instant we both reacted and pinned both arms of the man, but in doing so, all three of us toppled forward down the stairs, landing in a heap. Fortunately the uniform sergeant had by now moved out of the way and we were still able to restrain the man and propel him straight into the cells.

Apparently a brother of the man had been arrested for violent behaviour and he thought he would get him out of the police station by creating havoc. He had entered the public area, jumped over the charge room counter, brushing aside the duty constable and floored the duty sergeant who had tried to stop him.

As it was Sunday and court day on the Monday, I decided to keep him in the cells overnight and, before going off duty, typed up a précis of the events for the court the next day.

The next morning our chief inspector happened to read my report and questioned me as to whether I had cautioned the man during the melee.

"Yes, I did," said I.

"What did you say, Roger?"

"Mind the bloody step."

A week before Christmas, a local businessman called at the station to report that an oven-ready turkey he had hanging in the garage had disappeared. He was able to state that the only person who had called between the relevant times to when the turkey was taken was the coalman, who delivered half a ton of coal to his address.

During the course of enquiries, it was revealed that the

coalman was no less than one of our local petty criminals. His previous criminal history was unknown to his employer. Armed with this information, I sent a couple of constables to interview him and search his home.

A blank was drawn as he didn't admit to the theft and a search of his home revealed no stolen property.

A month or so after Christmas, I had occasion to arrest the coalman for stealing from his employer by manipulating the loads. Whilst he was in custody, I decided to raise the question of the missing turkey with him. He admitted the theft and when I asked where the turkey was when the constables searched his house, he started to laugh and said, "The turkey was in the oven, ready to cook. The missus and I burst out laughing when they left." A lesson learnt there.

Brian had become the joker of the station and on one occasion when an office constable developed Bell's palsy, a note appeared on the noticeboard to the effect that the constable had to drop out of the West Penwith Whistling championships.

The woman police inspector came to our office one winter's morning wearing a long coat with a rather nice broach of two little birds on the collar. Brian, again without thinking, said, "What a lovely pair of blue tits you have, ma'am." The woman inspector's face went crimson and she made a hasty exit from the office.

We had a spate of house burglaries which followed the same pattern; house ransacked and then the offender would defecate in one of the rooms. We eventually recovered some stolen property which led us to the offender. He was a well-known fifty-year-old evil person who had no respect for anyone or any living thing. In his first night in the cells, he blocked the cell toilet and kept flushing it until he flooded his cell and everything else on that floor. He refused to unblock the toilet so Chippy donned a pair of marigolds and did the job. Chippy then took the prisoner's shoes and dipped them in the toilet and left them outside the cell door soaking overnight.

The next morning we went to court to ask for a remand in custody of the prisoner, and as he walked across the courtroom, all we could hear was squelch, squelch, squelch, coming from his shoes. He entered the box facing the magistrates and immediately put up his hand.

The chairman of the bench nodded to him and asked what he wanted. The prisoner said, "I want to make a complaint."

"What about?" said the magistrate.

"Those two over there," said he, pointing to us.

I whispered to Chippy, "We're in for it now. It's the bloody shoes."

"What is your complaint?" asked the magistrate.

"They wouldn't give me a fag."

The magistrate addressed me and said, "Mr Harvey, would you see that the prisoner gets a cigarette."

"Yes, sir," I replied.

Chippy whispered, "Get one out of the toilet."

We had a call one morning from a local antique dealer, who had a shop in the centre of the city, to the effect that earlier he had sold a silver teapot to a Chinese man who paid by cheque. The dealer had gone straight to his bank and subsequently found that the cheque was a stolen one. We circulated a description immediately to the force area and then did a quick search of Truro taxi ranks, bus station and railway station. As soon as I returned to the police station, Chippy was coming out in a rush. A call had been received from the station master to the effect that after I had left the railway station, a Chinaman had appeared and was now sitting on the London train which was to leave shortly. We dashed up to the railway station, crossed over the line to where the station master indicated as to where the man was sitting. He informed us that he could only hold the train for one minute longer. Chippy asked the Chinese man to open his suitcase, once we had identified ourselves, but he refused. We took him off the train and back to the police station and placed him in an interview room. We had got verification from the Metropolitan Police that the cheque was one from a book stolen in a house burglary. We were ready to do the interview and in the room with the Chinese man, when the switchboard operator knocked on the door saying there was an urgent call for CID concerning the Chinese man. I took the call from Liskeard CID which was to say, "We've just caught your Chinaman here in Liskeard with the teapot." It turned out the man we had was on his way to Portsmouth to take an important exam that day and now there was no way he could get there by public transport.

So with the help of other forces, we shipped him out in a patrol car and by changing cars every so often, managed to get him to his destination. We didn't hear anything more or receive a complaint about this matter.

There was a uniform sergeant at Truro who was always trying to give up smoking but never quite managing it. He knew I kept cigarettes in my desk drawer for prisoners when required. He was always asking for cigarettes but never replacing them. One day I bought some joke bangers that could be stuffed into cigarettes and I filled the whole packet with them. Weeks must have passed and I forgot about them. One day, sergeants and inspectors were summoned to a meeting by the district commander. The sergeant in question was attending the meeting and asked to borrow a cigarette. I had really forgotten the banger inserts. Everybody was allowed to smoke if they wished because the district commander was a pipe smoker. The talk had started and several present were smoking. Suddenly there was an almighty bang as the cigarette the sergeant was smoking exploded. He had tobacco all over his face and over the head of the officer sitting in front of him. I kept quiet and saw Chippy out of the corner of my eye and he winked. After the meeting was over, I was trying to explain that it wasn't done on purpose but no one believed me.

Roger J took a call from the Metropolitan Police one day, in respect of a raid they had carried out and had come across a number of nude photographs of a lady who lived in Truro.

Although the photographs were not hard porn, I thought a visit to the Truro address may well find out something else. Roger J and I visited the small terraced house in the centre of Truro. We walked up the narrow path and Roger J reached the door first and knocked. I was standing behind him. The door was opened by a small, young man and before anything could be said a Siamese cat flew out of the door into the arms of Roger, sinking its claws into his nice white shirt and into his chest. His white shirt was now rapidly colouring red from the blood caused by the cat's claws. The young man grabbed hold of the cat and then grabbed hold of a second cat who looked as if he were going to try the same trick. We were invited in and immediately saw across the living room ceiling scores of photographs of a very pretty woman. We heard footsteps coming down the stairs and there she was, the young lady in the photographs. The young man and lady were not in the least embarrassed by our presence. Roger J explained the purpose of our visit. The young man just said, "Look, as far as we are concerned, it is just art and we supply art-type magazines with the photos. We only do it so we can make enough money to set up an art studio."

We left them and returned to the police station with Roger J wearing his red shirt. As we entered the station, we met the duty uniform inspector coming out. "What has happened to you?" he asked.

"Got attacked by a lion, sir."

"I'm sure," said the inspector. "Another one of one's fairy tales."

Mr Osborne had now gone and newly promoted Detective Chief Inspector Warren arrived. The police house he took over had a large garden and Mr Warren wanted a lawn mower. Someone told him that I knew where second-hand mowers could be bought from a chap in Chacewater village. I had previously met Mr Jose, the secondhand mower man, after he had reported a young man crawling around his garden one night eating his daffodils. It turned out the young man was a retired police officer's son who was high on drugs. I took Mr Warren to see Mr Jose, who, amongst other things was a retired farmer, to see the grass machines. There was a shed containing about fifty lawn mowers of every description. Mr Warren walked up and down the rows of machines. "How old is this one?" asked Mr Warren and he repeated the question another dozen times in respect of other machines. We had been there about an hour by then and Mr Warren once again said, "And how old is this one?"

Mr Jose said, "Look here, captain, I don't have the birth certificates of these, you know."

Mr Warren didn't buy one.

There was a scrap metal dealer in Truro city who at times was a pain in the backside with some of things he tried on the public. A likeable rogue who died rather suddenly one morning. Within an hour of his funeral, the story was doing the rounds of the pubs he had visited that when he arrived at the Pearly Gates and announced he was a scrap man, Saint Peter told him to wait whilst he made a few enquiries to see if he could be admitted. When Saint Peter returned a few minutes later, the scrap man had gone and so had the gates.

I had a call one day from a local businessman who ran a large company employing a number of people and asked if I could attend a boardroom meeting with him later that day as they had uncovered a large fraud within the company. Later that day, I visited his premises and was surprised to see his solicitor and bank manager also present. It seemed that his office secretary of thirty years had been taking money from the company which now amounted to a very large sum. After going over everything, it looked quite a clear-cut fraud. The secretary had been suspended from work the previous day on advice from the solicitor.

The next day, I visited a local caravan park where the lady secretary resided and introduced myself. She was very polite and invited me in. I put the allegation to her and I was completely taken aback when she admitted taking the money and also stated that she had it all in her bank account and hadn't spent a penny of it. Before I could say anything else, she said, "I can see you are surprised but, you see, I have worked for the company since leaving school and in all that time I have done the wages for the staff. I was instructed by the chairman that no tax would be paid on any overtime worked by any member of the staff. You can imagine how much, over the last thirty years, this has amounted to." I could see where she was coming from and excused myself after saying further enquiries would be made.

I telephoned the chairman and arranged a meeting, advising him to have the same bank manager and solicitor present. The next day, I met with all three again and related what the lady secretary had told me. I could tell from the look on the faces of the bank manager and solicitor that they were quite surprised by what I had told them. I left them to it and the next day I had a call from the chairman, withdrawing the complaint. Years later, I learned that the lady had moved out of the caravan park and was living in a nice little bungalow.

CHAPTER 12

Rossannagh and I had bought a farm property in the village of Mullion on the Lizard Peninsular, where we kept two horses and our dogs, Bede, a Jack Russell, and Drum, a hound cross bull terrier. How we came to have these two dogs was that, on one particular day, I was making theft enquiries outside the village of Chacewater and had called at a farm in connection with the enquiry. As I entered the farmyard, I saw the farmer with a shotgun under his arm. I asked what he was doing and he went on the explain that he bred pure bull terriers and that the local hunt had crossed his land when one of the bull terrier bitches was in season. The result was thirteen puppies were born. He had disposed of twelve but had kept one back to take the milk of the mother but now no longer had any use for the pup and was going to shoot it. I asked to see the pup and ended up buying it from him. He wanted to give it to me but I insisted on paying to make it legal. The farmer would only accept

£1. On the way home with the pup, I called at another farm and bought Bede, a Jack Russell, for £3.

One fine morning, I left the stable yard at the Grange on my horse and rode along the bridle path which passed through my neighbour's farm. The farmer had, the previous day, brought contractors onto his land to dig a new septic tank pit to take the slurry from his Shippon. The pit, having been dug, was some fifteen feet deep, square in shape with very sheer walls and as I rode by, I could see over the hedge into the pit. I was somewhat surprised to see a large fox at the bottom of the pit running in circles. It appeared to have fallen in as the pit had been dug on the line the fox was used to following each night.

I rode on to the next farm, where I knew a keen hunt foot follower would be. Having found the man, I then rode back to the pit and waited until the man arrived with his tractor. He took a rope, made a noose and lowered it into the pit and with a flick of the wrist, caught the fox in the noose and quickly pulled it up to the surface. Then, at speed, grabbed the fox by the scruff of its neck and released the noose and then let it go. The fox took off across the fields to live another day.

On another occasion the local hunt met at the Grange. It was a good turnout of horses, riders and foot followers, and joining the hunt for the first time was a taxi driver from Truro, together with his wife. An aunt had died and left them some money so they had decided to buy a couple of horses, having had a few riding lessons. As they rode up to join the other riders, it was noticeable that the man had his riding hat perched on the back of his head, a lit cigarette in his mouth and his riding crop stuck in his boot. The horn sounded and the hunt took off with a run of about a mile, then stopped upon losing the fox's scent. It was at this point that I was privy to hear the master of the hounds (a very well-spoken man) call the taxi driver over to him and say, "My man, the cry is 'tally-ho', not 'follow the fucking fox'."

The same Master of Hounds, on another occasion, rode over to a hunt foot follower who had seen a three-legged fox travelling up a gully out of sight of the hunt. The hunt follower had got excited and was shouting to attract the hound's attention. The master, in his authoritative voice, said, "My man, there is no need to shout. I have a horn, a whistle and a voice."

"Well," said the hunt follower, "I wish you would use one of the buggers."

We had a spate of break-ins in the city centre, mainly in clothing shops and during the early hours of one morning, I was called and informed that the Littlewoods store in the city centre had been broken in to and it was thought the offenders were still inside. I sped to the scene and joined the rest of our team. We could hear the offenders on the roof of the large building, who, in spite of calls to give themselves up, remained at large. I shouted, "If you don't come down, we will send the dogs up the fire escape." There was still no reply to my call after a few minutes, so I called loudly, "Release the dogs."

On that cue, Chippy started barking very convincingly,

which was interrupted almost immediately by one of the offenders calling in a hysterical voice, "Don't send the dogs. We will come down."

Three arrests were made and several other break-ins were cleared up in admissions by the three.

Opposite Littlewoods was another ladies' outfitters and I had a two a.m. call from the duty sergeant informing me that the store had been broken in to by a female who had smashed the plate glass window and who was sitting in the display area. I met the sergeant outside the shop and together we climbed through the broken window into the display area. The lady was now trying on a fur coat and it was obvious she had been drinking. Together we managed to get here out of the shop window into the street. She now started to fight in a drunken way and in our attempt to get her into the back of the police van, the sergeant managed to pull the right arm off the coat. Several months later, we were called to a house in Truro, where the same woman had been stabbed some twenty times by her boyfriend following a drunken row. Miraculously, she survived to tell the tale.

In a secure compound on the edge of the city, a Ford dealer kept new cars before being displayed in a city centre showroom. Staff arriving at the compound discovered the main gate had been forced and a brand new, unregistered, pink Ford Corsair was missing. Numerous enquiries were made to no avail. Some twelve months after the theft of the car, we were carrying out a search of a property in the village of St Agnes, following the arrest of the owner for shoplifting. To our surprise, when searching an outhouse, we found the Ford Corsair. The car had been stolen from the compound, driven about ten miles to St Agnes, placed in the shed and never used again. The thief, having taken the car, was then afraid to use it as it was the only pink Corsair in the county.

The River Fal that ran from Truro down to the sea at Falmouth, was, in places, a deep water mooring for cruise ships that were laid up for various reasons. Two large cruise ships had been at anchor below the King Harry ferry for several months and we were quite surprised one morning to have a call from the shipping agent to the effect that a large organ had been taken from each of the ship's ballrooms over a period of four days. A night watchman was responsible for security but he couldn't remember specific times he had checked the ballrooms of each ship.

The enquiries were commenced and a number of persons on shore had seen lights at the sides of the ships and objects being lowered onto rafts. It didn't take long to uncover a local man who was involved in setting up the theft, resulting in the two organs being recovered from Penzance where they had been sold to a local dealer.

New probationary constables, when on night duty in the Lemon Street area of Truro, were asked by control to look out for a stoned man near the inn at the top of the street. This was of course a prank to be played on the unsuspecting constables as the stoned man was the statue of Richard Lander, a famous son of Truro.

One of the uniformed sergeants at Truro was Harold Thompson, six feet five, nineteen stone and a real Cornish character. Always up for a joke or a bit of play acting. One morning as I entered the first floor, Harold at the other end of the corridor shouted, "Right, Harvey, rugby tackle coming up," at the same time charging towards me. I immediately bent down to avoid him catching hold of me but stood up again too quickly, catching Harold off balance, resulting in him flying over my shoulder and crashing to the floor. He lay very still in a stupor but fortunately recovered fairly quickly. He swore blind that I had done it on purpose and vowed that he would pay me back in some way.

A few days later, I was driving a CID car through the centre of Truro accompanied by one of the department's constables. As I approached the traffic lights in the city centre, the lights were red as the streets and pavements were very busy with pedestrians. As the lights changed to green, I engaged first gear to drive off when suddenly, from nowhere, Harold appeared in full uniform in front of the car and, without warning, opened my driver's door and dragged me out to the front of the car. I was too surprised to do anything other than to be held by Harold in a vice-like grip. By now, members of the public had started to congregate and stare in awe at what was happening. Harold was now in full voice, shouting to the crowd not to worry as the man he was holding had stolen a car. My passenger, instead of coming to my aid, had got out and walked back to the police station. Harold was now in his element, entertaining the crowd with traffic backed up behind the CID car. It was then that someone in the crown recognised me and called out, "It's Sergeant Harvey he's got, he's a copper too."

Harold turned to me and said, "I'll give you a caution this time, but you'd better behave yourself in future."

I got back into the car and as I drove off, I could see him in the mirror, still entertaining the crowd with his usual trick of putting his thumb in his mouth whilst his back was to the wall, blowing and making his helmet rise. I never met anyone who didn't love or respect Harold.

Our department had a dedicated typist who was a devout Roman Catholic, and, following a number of arrests for gross indecency in public toilets in the city, she was given the file statements to type.

Having reached one particular statement in the bundle, she came rather hurriedly into the office. She appeared very flustered. I asked if something was wrong to which she replied, "I buy my pasties from this man and I'm disgusted."

At that moment I was joined by Chippy and I explained about the pasties. Chippy looked at me and winked then said, "Can you remember what he was doing when we arrested him?"

I said, "Yes, he was using false teeth to crimp the pasty edges."

Mrs R, the typist, looked at Chippy and asked if what I had said was true.

Chippy, with a straight face, said, "Yes, but not only that, you should see how he puts the holes on the doughnuts!"

Mrs R fled from the office and ran across to the nearby Catholic church. It was some half hour before she returned.

Whilst on the same subject, I had the unfortunate duty of arresting one of our uniformed constables who had been committing acts of gross indecency whilst on patrol. He was convicted and sent to prison for a short period of time and on his release, having been discharged from the force, returned to Truro and paraded in the town dressed in a white suit and a handbag.

One of the last working tin mines in Cornwall was the Wheal Jane and it was situated in our division; we were responsible for safety storage checks on the dynamite.

I had a call one day from the mine manager who reported that several sticks of dynamite were missing since the explosive store had last been checked. Enquiries commenced and each of the miners' employment records were looked in to. Suspicion fell on one particular man who had come from the coal industry in South Wales. A call to my opposite number in South Wales revealed that he was related to a person they suspected of being involved in a number of burglaries in which explosives was used on safes.

At about the same time, we had two good class houses broken into quite near the mine. Cash was stolen from one and a collection of antique firearms taken from the other.

I decided it was time to pay the miner a visit and that evening I drove to the town of Redruth where he rented a terraced house and resided with his girlfriend.

In answer to my knock, the door was opened by the miner and I introduced myself. He immediately became abusive so I informed him that I was arresting him on suspicion of burglary and taking him to Truro. Without further warning, he smashed himself against the inner door of the passageway, thereby releasing the door from its hinges, such was his temper.

To prevent any further damage to him or me, I grabbed hold of his arm and forced him onto the passage floor, handcuffing his hands behind his back. I then got him to his feet, out of the door and into the front passenger seat of my car. After a few miles, we reached the village of Chacewater, by which time he had calmed down and wanted to talk. He asked if I was going to get him remanded to Exeter prison and I replied that it depended on answers I got from him. He asked me to stop the car and I pulled into a layby.

He said, "My girlfriend is pregnant and she will be very worried about what is going to happen."

"Providing I have all the answers, then there would be no reason to keep you in custody."

"OK, drive me out to the mine."

This I did and it was eleven p.m. on a very dark night by the time I drove up to the mine. I stopped and unfastened his handcuffs and then, quick as a flash, he was out of the car and gone into the darkness before I could utter a word.

I thought he had done a runner but decided to sit and wait to see what would happen.

About ten minutes later, to my relief, he returned to the car with his arms full with the stolen antique guns.

I drove him to Truro where he admitted the burglaries and also the theft of the dynamite. When asked how he had got the explosive out of the mine without being detected, he said that he would place a stick of dynamite in his empty tea flask at the end of his shift, making it virtually undetectable.

He was given bail as promised and months later both he and his cousin from Wales were given terms of imprisonment.

I had a one a.m. call from a young promotion-minded uniform sergeant who was the night duty sergeant at Truro. He was most apologetic on the phone, stating he had a situation in which he didn't know what to do. I sat up in bed and listened to what he had to say.

Apparently, a senior officer had been out celebrating and had been dropped off at the police station where he had a few drinks in the station police club. He was now in the lift and for over three quarters of an hour had been riding between the ground and fourth floors without getting out.

After listening to this I said, "When the lift comes down to your floor, grab hold of him and throw him in the cells for the night."

There was a gasp at the end of the phone followed by, "I can't do that, it will ruin my career."

I laughed and said, "I'll come down." Within half an hour I was at the station and met the sergeant who was now in a state of anxiety, coupled with the jitters.

As the lift came down to the first floor, the doors opened and there was a very jolly, inebriated officer. I glanced round and noticed that the sergeant had disappeared. I stepped into the lift and heaved the now slumped figure up and propelled him down the station ramp and into my car.

I drove him home and woke his wife and together we got him into the house.

The next morning, I had a knock on my office door, which then opened and a very apologetic man poked his head around. "Sorry you had to be called out last night," said the head.

"That's all right, sir. Just don't make a habit of it," I replied.

As for the uniform sergeant, his career was saved and he went on and upwards in the ranks.

I had a visit one day from the headmaster of a prominent public school, who was very concerned about a sum of money that had been taken from his study over a period of forty-eight hours. Wishing to see where the money had gone missing, I accompanied him to the school and into his study. Pupils at the school had no access to the study so the theft had to have been committed by one of the dozen male teachers.

I interviewed all the teachers over the following couple of days and had taken possession of a brown paper bag from which the money had been stolen.

After the interviews, I felt fairly certain that it could have been between two of the teachers but I had no admissions.

With the headmaster's permission, I printed a notice which I placed in the teachers' common room for all to see.

I have today received the result of a forensic test on the brown paper bag and am now in possession of a set of prints believed to be that of the thief. I therefore intend to fingerprint all teachers in the next forty-eight hours, with a view to exposing the thief.

The next morning, I had a call from the headmaster, informing me that the stolen money had been returned. He asked if I still intended to fingerprint his staff but I had to tell him that the notice was a bluff as there never were any prints on the bag. Adding that it was my way of trying to provoke a reaction.

The same afternoon, the headmaster called to see me and to tell me that one of his teachers had resigned immediately and left the county. The man in question was one of the two I had suspected.

I was asked not to pursue the matter any further as the publicity of a prosecution against the teacher would have been bad public relations for the school.

In the late sixties, drugs were becoming more available in Cornwall and information had started coming from St

Mawes that drug abuse was rife amongst the kitchen staff of hotels in that area.

Relying on information from the St Mawes resident constable, I organised a team of uniform and plain clothes officers and early one morning carried out a series of raids. As a result, several hotel workers were arrested for possessing cannabis or LSD. I set up a temporary police station in the foyer of one of the hotels. As all the seized drugs had to be sent for forensic examination, bail was granted pending the result of the forensic tests.

A few days later, a report was received from one of the hotels that a large sum of money was missing from the hotel safe. Enquiries soon revealed that three kitchen porters had left their jobs overnight and purchased a second-hand car from a local garage.

Details of the car and three men were circulated nationwide and some four days later I received a call from a Lossiemouth police sergeant, who informed me that he had the three in custody awaiting collection. It didn't take long to realise that Lossiemouth was some eight hundred miles north of Truro and that five constables would have to be sent by train to collect them. I worked out the cost of wages, fares and accommodation for the escort and prisoners, after which I got a firm price for the hire of a six-seater plane from Exeter Air Services. It turned out the plane would make a considerable saving in time and money, so I got permission to hire the plane to fly from Newquay to Lossiemouth and return.

I had to draw lots in the office as everyone wanted to be

on the trip. Brian won and together we caught our evening flight from Newquay and a few hours later landed at Lossiemouth, where we were met on the runway by the Scottish sergeant and his staff, together with the three prisoners.

On seeing the small plane, one of the three started to protest that he suffered from a fear of flying and had no intention of getting on the plane. The Scottish sergeant looked at me and I winked at him. I then turned to the protesting prisoner and said, "What I am prepared to do, if my Scottish colleague agrees to hold you, is that I will knock you out and carry you aboard the plane, and with a bit of luck you will still be asleep when we arrive in Newquay."

The prisoner looked from me to the Scottish sergeant, neither of us smiled, and then he said, "Bugger that, I'll get on the plane."

We took off and in the early hours of the morning, landed safely at Newquay without further complaint from the prisoners.

Calling in at the police station one evening, I saw on entering the foyer an elderly couple seated. The man appeared to have a cut above his eye and the lady had been crying. I enquired from the duty sergeant what the problem was and he explained that the couple had an only child very late in life and that now as a seventeen-year-old he was making their lives a living hell. He refused to work and demanded money from them daily for drink and cigarettes.

Refusal resulted in violence towards the father, who could not defend himself against his brute of a son.

I asked the sergeant what was going to be done. He informed me that he had advised the couple that it was a civil family matter and they should consult a solicitor.

This didn't rest easy with me so I invited them into my office and got the full story from them, after which I told them of a course of action I was prepared to take with their co-operation.

At ten p.m. that night, I let myself into their house and sat in the kitchen and waited. Just after ten thirty, I heard a car pull up, a door slam and then drive away. A few moments later, the back door opened and a large figure stumbled into the kitchen, shouting, "Mother, get me something to eat. Now!" At that moment I turned on the light, which took him by surprise, and then grabbed hold of him and spun him around and propelled him out to my car, at the same time telling him who I was. I then drove to the station and placed him in a cell. He was now crying his eyes out. The cells in the old station were as bad as any in the force are and prisoners were always thankful to leave them.

The young man had now been in his cell for about two hours when I took him out and back to his home. His parents were in the kitchen in their dressing gowns in a very apprehensive state, and I invited the mother to make a pot of tea. I then laid the law down to the young man, pointing out that he had experienced what would happen to him if he didn't mend his ways. I instructed the parents and their son to be at Truro police at noon later that day.

At exactly noon, they arrived and I took them to my office I could see the son was still visibly shaken from his encounter with the cell. I said to the son, "Last night you told me you had an interest in the motor trade and this morning I have spoken to a garage proprietor who is prepared to give you a chance to learn the trade. Do you want the job?"

"Yes," he replied.

I said, "Well, I will warn you that the garage owner is a far tougher man than me, but providing you buckle down to work and treat your parents with the respect they deserve, then you will be treated fairly."

The young man took up the challenge and made a success of his life, and eventually married a local girl.

Several years later, when I was doing my mounted bit in Devon, I had a call from one of my old CID colleagues who, in passing, mentioned that the young man had called at Truro police station to see me. I don't know whether it was to thank me or knock my block off!

Whilst at Truro, I attended a fingerprint and handwriting course in Wakefield. Other courses were also being held at this force HQ, including a couple for police officers from remote parts of Africa. One evening in the club bar I got engaged in conversation with one of the class instructors, whose expertise was in fingerprint identification. He started telling me about a police chief he had in his class at that time who, in spite of all the tuition, could on the comparison test only bring the identification down to three suspects. The police chief was delighted with his result in spite of the instructors frustration, and when asked why the delight by the instructor, he was informed that the police chief from whom he was taking over when he returned to Africa could only get it down to five suspects. When asked how to identify the suspect from the three, he was informed that all three would, where necessary, be put to death.

Now that, I thought, was real zero tolerance policing.

I returned to the station at about midnight one evening with George, having dealt with a theft. At the same time, a member of the public entered the station and was relating what he had just witnessed on Lemon Quay. The duty sergeant was out of the station assisting at an accident. What had been witnessed was a group of yobs playing football with a constable's helmet, the constable being unable to do anything. I ascertained that the constable on town patrol was a young probationer who had only been at Truro for about four or five weeks. I informed the civilian clerk that George and I would go to the constable's aid. The constable hadn't radioed in so it was possible his radio may also have been taken.

We left the station and walked the short distance to Lemon Quay and on arrival could see five or six of our local criminal element sitting on the wall above the River Fal and opposite the burger van. The young constable was pleading with them to give his helmet back to no avail other than jeers. The helmet was being passed from one to the other like a game of pass the parcel. As we approached, I called asking for the helmet to be given back but this fell on deaf ears.

I noticed that the tide was out, revealing gleaming mud in the glare of the street lights. The drop from the wall to the mud was only a matter of feet so without hesitation, I caught the two ringleaders in their chests simultaneously with the flat of my hands. The result was that both went backwards over the wall and lay sprawling in the river mud. The other members of the group had now jumped off the wall to avoid the same treatment. I told them to go to the aid of the two in the mud and advised the whole group that any further disrespect to the police of Truro would be dealt with more severely. The young constable was a bit shaken and obviously embarrassed. However, I was able to reassure him that he would have no further trouble. At the same time I advised him not to follow my example.

In 2008, whilst attending the Royal Cornwall Show at Wadebridge, I saw the same two who had met their fate in the mud of the River Fal. These two, now in their sixties, were sitting on the grass outside the beer tent and on seeing me, the first one said, "Hello, Mr Harvey, still got a few horses?" We had a bit of a chat about the show and I bought them a couple of pints. Between the pair they had shared several terms of imprisonment over the years but there was no animosity between us because they understood the rules of the game. That night, punishment was meted out, no arrests made, justice was done.

Truro was, at times, a haven for shoplifters with one of the main targets being Woolworths. We knew the management team at the store really well as there was always a couple of arrests each week without fail. One day in conversation with the store manager, he mentioned about suspicions he had about a man that came into the store every Saturday morning. The man was always dressed in the same long overcoat and carried a holdall in each hand but never made a purchase from the store. The manager was sure the man was up to something but didn't know what. I asked the manager to give our department a call when the man was in the store again, adding that we would take a look at him.

The following Saturday, a call was received and I went to the store with one of our team and once having had the man pointed out, kept observation on him. For the next thirty minutes, the man wandered from counter to counter making no purchase. His manner was enough to cause suspicion with his continual furtive looks. I decided to have a word with him and, after identification, took him to a side office in the store. The man made no protest at being detained and I asked him to put down his bags. He stated that he couldn't because inside the sleeves of his overcoat he had two false arms. The hands of the false arms had gloves on, which in turn were fitted perfectly into the handles of his holdalls. His real arms and hands inside the overcoat were free to shoplift from inside his coat. Inside the coat were poacher's pockets full of stolen items. A search of his house produced hundreds of pounds of stolen goods.

On the eastern side of Truro was a block of police houses and most of the residents kept their gardens in good order apart from one constable who was bone idle when it came to gardening. His garden was completely disgusting with lawn grass, in some places, over two feet high. The chief inspector had spoken to him about doing something but the advice was ignored. A report somehow reached the district commander's desk, reiterating the complaint and ending with 'The grass in this man's garden is so long I have to send my cat out with a packed lunch in case it cannot find its way back'. The grass was soon done.

A clothing parade was held each year at most police stations for new uniforms and on one occasion the clothing lorry arrived at Truro and parked in the police station car park. All the constables lined up to have their measurements taken and in the queue was Jack and, unfortunately for him, behind him was John, the station's biggest practical joker. Jack's measurement for trousers and an overcoat were taken, after which the tailor's attention was diverted, giving John the opportunity to pick up a pen and alter the tailor's writing on Jack's order form. He took ten inches off the length of his trousers and put twelve inches on his coat.

Six months later, the new uniforms arrived and inspection carried out. Jack had trousers which finished at his calf and a coat that came within an inch of the floor. No one could figure out what had happened at the time but it came to light when Jack retired.

During the course of three months, we collated some thirty complaints of one of our famous Gypsy families having obtained scrap metal by false pretences, or in other words, not having paid anyone. Armed with complaints, I decided to visit the camp site to see the man in question. He was a notorious character who had spent almost as long in prison as he had out. As I approached the camp, a patrol car came out of the site and the driver immediately recognised me and flagged me down, pulling alongside. He asked if I was going into the site and when I told him who I was going to see, he said, "We've just tried to see his son but we were ordered out. There's about twenty dogs roaming in there and not all of them friendly."

I asked if they had seen the chap I was looking for. The answer was that he was in his caravan with his wife who was unwell. He wished me the best of luck and drove off.

I decided to leave my car outside the camp and walk in. I was immediately surrounded by dogs and as I walked through the site, I was lucky not to be bitten as I reached the caravan I wanted. The door opened and my man came out with a shotgun under his arm. We had met several times before so he was well aware who I was. "What do you want?" he said.

I replied, "I was out this way and heard that your wife was poorly so I thought I would drop in to see how she was."

"Come in and have a cup of tea," he said.

I entered the caravan to see his wife in bed. I spent the next hour talking about everything under the sun – dogs, horses, people, the council and so on. I then said, "By the way, now I'm here, you've been a bit naughty, because they tell me back at the station you have been visiting people and getting scrap metal and, after promising to pay, haven't done so."

He said, "Are you dealing with it or are they coming out to arrest me?"

"What do you want to do? I only called to see how your wife was."

"Let's get it over with, are you going to arrest me?"

"What, and leave your poor wife to look after herself? What I can do is go to my car and ring in to get the details and take it from there."

I went to my car and got my briefcase, in which I had the details. I had no way of contacting anybody. We didn't have radios or mobile phones in those days.

I returned to the caravan after a decent wait and ran through all the complaints, after which he made a statement under caution, admitting each of the offences and I informed him the matter would be reported. I told him that I hoped his wife would soon be up and about and thanked him for the tea. He shook my hand and thanked me for calling. A few months later, having been summoned to attend Truro magistrate's court, he was sentenced to six months' imprisonment.

Several months later, his son was sentenced to six months' imprisonment for theft of metal. After the court hearing, the son was in Truro police station cells awaiting escort to Exeter Prison, when the father, who had himself just been released from prison, called at the station asking to see his son before being carted off. The duty sergeant was a bit worried about letting them meet and called for me to make a decision.

I confronted the father, who assured me that all he wanted to do was say goodbye to his son and give him some sweets. I walked him into the cell corridor and opened the cell door whereupon, the father charged past me, grabbed hold of his son and started to beat seven bells out of him, shouting, "What have I told you about stealing?"

I managed to separate them and calm the father down. Talk about the kettle calling the pot black. It did cross my mind that, by the utterance, 'what have I told you about stealing' did he mean 'you're not supposed to get caught'?

The new police station was now complete and we all moved in, including the district commander and his deputy.

Truro subdivision was made up of several villages and hamlets stretching from Perranporth on the north coast to St Mawes on the south, and between Truro and St Mawes was the village of Tregony, where a sergeant resided with responsibility for the country area. A new sergeant had arrived to this posting, a man who had been a constable for over twenty years and was used to his own country station beat and way of life.

A court was held in Tregony church hall once a month, presided over by a local magistrate with the chairman being a local lady landowner. The new sergeant hadn't been established very long before everyone realised that his favourite word was the 'F' word. It was not spoken in an abusive manner but just as a normal person would use 'and' or 'it'. It was obviously everyday use for him and it slipped out in court a few times and he had to be cautioned for his choice of words.

A young constable stationed at St Mawes met the sergeant on the quayside one sunny morning and it wasn't long before the constable's wife, with their new born baby, was seen coming towards them. The sergeant hadn't seen the new baby before and as the constable's wife reached them, the sergeant greeted the wife and then peered into the pram and said, "What a beautiful baby. What do you feed the fucker on?"

The top floor of the new station was taken up with the offices for the district commander and his deputy, Mr Jenkins. Mr Jenkins dropped into my office one morning for something or other and asked if I had seen the top floor offices. I hadn't, so he invited me up. He took me into the district commander's office, which was spacious and had a rather nice toilet suite. He then showed me his office, which was also palatial but no toilet suite. I asked why he didn't have a loo like the district commander. Mr Jenkins replied, "I didn't qualify because he's a bigger shit than me!"

CHAPTER 13

Rossanagh and I had turned the Grange farmhouse into a small hotel with bathrooms added on each bedroom. The sitting room was enormous with sea views and the dining room with a view over farmland. We had also purchased a three bedroom cottage on the edge of the farm for holiday lets, and Rossanagh ran the business with the help of part-time staff.

This was the future, a good business, horses, dogs and chickens, and then one day I returned home unexpectedly and found that Rossanagh was having an affair with a young chap from the village. The situation became intolerable so I flew to Holland and sold the whole property to some Dutch friends. At about the same time I bumped into Joy in Truro. I had previously met her and her husband many years before when I was at Plymouth Hospital. We had all met a few times and they had visited the Grange a couple of times. In conversation I mentioned that I was looking for somewhere to put the horses. Joy explained that her husband was selling his business and had a boat built and intended to sail to America. She was unsure what was going to happen at Penvale farm where they lived but I could keep the horses there for the time being. I moved into lodgings and the horses moved to Penvale. I have never, from that day, seen Rossanagh, but I did visit her mother a few times when in the Exmoor area where she lived.

After a few months, Joy's husband made it plain that he was going to America and wanted to sell Penvale, leaving Joy and her two children undecided as to what to do. Planning permission had been granted on a stone barn on Penvale farm so, after some thought, I decided to purchase Joy's husband's half of the holding with the intention of converting the barn into accommodation for myself. I had a good bank manager in those days and the deal was done.

Joy was an open, honest person and I believe still very much in love with her husband. I know for a fact that when he wanted to sail off to America he had advertised for female crew; Joy offered to let him go for five years, during which time she would run his business so that he could get whatever it was out of his system. He, however, had other ideas and a divorce followed. He had been leading a bit of a double life, which was distressing for her when it came to light.

One of the horses I had was a promising mare which I put into training as a hurdler with Mrs Elizabeth Kennard, a respected West Country trainer and had the pleasure of seeing the mare run at Newton Abbot a few times. The mare ran under the name of Penvale Member, Penvale being the name of the farm and Member being part of the sire's name, New Member.

On a day off from work, I was at Newton Abbot Racecourse when I ran into a group of officers from headquarters, which included the deputy chief constable and a former Cornish officer I had served with. I passed the time of day and quickly moved on but was later caught in the saddling enclosure by the Cornishman, who had spotted my name in the programme as the owner and wanted to know if the mare was going to win. I told him I had no idea. When the race was called and the horses set off, the mare was doing well and leading the field, but a short distance from the winning post, a saddle strap broke, causing the saddle to slip back and suddenly the race was over for Penvale Member.

It was getting expensive to keep a horse in training and an opportunity arose for me to sell her. The mare's name was changed and she went on to do very well under the new owner. I had two more young thoroughbred mares at home but didn't put these into training.

Joy had a Shih Tzu puppy called GB that used the cat flap in the farmhouse to come and go. One day a neighbouring farmer came into the yard alleging that GB had killed his ducklings. GB was such a gentle, friendly little dog and where the neighbour kept the ducklings was some two fields away, so he couldn't possibly have been the culprit.

A couple of months later, I bought a dozen ducklings and put them in a new house and run. A few days later, after morning coffee in the farmhouse, GB came in through the cat flap with his mouth covered in blood. A quick examination confirmed it wasn't his blood but a check outside revealed that he had been busy digging under the pen and having got in, killed all of the ducklings. I did go and see the neighbour and pay for his loss! Little GB had turned into the first fox-cum-Shih Tzu, but in spite of this he was still very much loved.

A police cavalcade was held in Truro one year and four police horses were brought down from the Birmingham force to take part. I had been approached about stabling them at Penvale. The horses arrived and were stabled and then the Birmingham chaps took off to Truro, leaving me to do the feeding and general looking after. I didn't mind as horses always figured somewhere in my life.

In the lounge at Penvale, Joy had a grand piano which was espied by one of the Birmingham mounted constables when they came in for coffee the next morning and he asked permission to play it. We listened to some wonderful playing over the next thirty minutes as it turned out the constable, prior to joining the police, was a concert pianist. You never know what hidden talent there is in the police.

A very famous horse was also stabled for two nights at Penvale and his name was Red Rum. He was doing a promotional tour of Cornwall.

When he had been unloaded and stabled, I asked one of the handlers if someone was going to look after him during the night. The handler said he'd be a bit difficult to handle and invited me to go into the box with the horse. This I did and could immediately see what he meant as the horse straight away showed his teeth and put his ears back in warning. I suspect it was the behaviour that made him the winner he was.

A murder enquiry had started at Falmouth, in which a businessman was suspected of killing his wife. Her body had been found at the water's edge and it was a question whether she had drowned or had been murdered prior to having been found in the sea. There was also the question as to whether the husband had been violent towards her in the past and as they had only moved from Herefordshire to Cornwall in the last few months, it was imperative to get the full background of what, if anything, at their previous address. The person who had all the answers was a countryman in Hereford who knew the family well, but he didn't want to get involved. I was therefore asked to travel up to see him to try to persuade him otherwise.

I caught the train up to Hereford and was collected by a CID sergeant and the next morning driven to the country estate of the man who would have all the answers. I hadn't made an appointment and was informed by the man's wife that he was just about to leave the stable yard to exercise his horses. We were directed to the yard where two very nice hunters had been saddled by a groom. With that, a colonel type man appeared and demanded to know what we wanted. This was my man. I introduced myself whereupon he immediately said that he had informed the local constabulary that he didn't want to get involved. I didn't say anything but walked around the two horses and expressed how nice they were and ran my hand down the flank of one. The man said, "Know anything about horses, do you?"

"Just a little."

"How little?"

So I expanded a little on what I had done. He seemed very interested in this Cornishman and said, "Would you like to ride with me?"

I pointed to my suit I was wearing and indicated I was not dressed for riding. He said, "A good horseman can ride in anything." I climbed aboard the hunter, he offered to drop me back at the police station after the ride rather than keep the detective sergeant, who was driving, hanging about.

We rode for a good couple of hours and talked about everything under the sun in connection with horses. We eventually returned to his manor house where he invited me in for a bite to eat, after which he offered to give me everything I wished to know in connection with my enquiry. The ride and talk had paid dividends as it certainly clarified the situation in Falmouth.

Funnily, when I entered the general CID office after my ride, scrawled across the blackboard was a message, 'Would the Lone Ranger please call his detective superintendent at the Falmouth incident room'.

Situated just outside Truro was a large country estate which was broken into one night and a large quantity of silver stolen. An examination of the scene revealed that some of the silver had been dropped on the lawn as the thieves made their getaway. Track marks in a field behind the main house indicated that two vehicles had been hidden in the field the night of the break-in. Telephone and alarm wires had been cut. On the day prior to the night of the burglary, three jewellery shops in Truro city had pads of expensive rings stolen by a gang of at least four people, so our department was fully stretched in trying to trace the offenders.

I had drawn a blank on the country house, it had been open to the public the previous week and a lot of people had passed through. A blank had been drawn on the jewellery apart from the descriptions. I myself had made three visits to one of the robbed shops and on the third visit implored the girl assistant to try and remember if any of the four people had touched anything else in the shop which they hadn't taken with them. The young girl thought for a few moments and then pointed to the silver trophy on a back shelf. She had suddenly remembered that as two woman were looking at the tray of rings, a man asked to see the silver trophy. It was obviously a distraction move away from the rings.

I took the silver trophy, which upon examination revealed the fingerprints of a criminal from the Midlands, who was suspected of thefts from ten other country houses over the last twelve months. A further print was found on a silver spoon, indicating another member of the suspected gang.

Mr Wilmott, our detective superintendent, had asked to be kept informed and once he had details of what had been found, spoke to Detective Chief Superintendent Sharpe at force headquarters, at which Mr Wilmott and I had to attend as there had been two similar country estate burglaries in the Devon area.

At Exeter, there had been a promotion board held in the morning and a number of selected CID officers had been celebrating with the chief superintendent.

We all attended the crime conference and listened to addresses from officers who had attended the two other estate raids. I had to relate what I had discovered and after a couple of hours the meeting was coming to a close as all details had been aired. The chief superintendent spoke to me across the table and informed me I would have to stay in Exeter that night and coordinate everything. I explained that I had to go back to Truro that evening but the chief superintendent shouted me down and in so many words told me I was being ordered to stay. I think the promotion celebrations had got to him. I turned to Mr Wilmott and told him I was returning to Truro that evening and would return to Exeter next morning. Mr Wilmott said that Mr Sharpe wouldn't be happy with that and if I rode home with him, he was liable to get into trouble for disobeying Mr Sharpe. I said, "Don't worry, I'll catch a train home."

It's funny how things turn out, because Mr Wilmott, who was a really nice chap, got into a drinking session with

Mr Sharpe and I ended up driving Mr Wilmott home to Truro in his car as I hadn't touched a drop of drink whereas Mr Wilmott was unfit to drive.

I drove up to Exeter the next day and coordinated the crimes, raids were in the Midlands and arrests were made, following which several people were convicted.

A few days after the convictions, I had a call from the office counter in the Truro police station that there was a butler from the estate which had been burgled wishing to see me. I went down to the first floor where the butler presented me with a brace of pheasant from the estate owner as a mark of appreciation. I also had a visit from the chief superintendent who apologised for his behaviour on that day. Adding that it was a job well done.

The barn conversion at Penvale had now been completed into two rather nice flats but had taken more money than catered for, so we decided to sell the whole lot. That is farmhouse, stables and land. It think it may have been a relief to Joy as memories of her ex-husband still lingered there.

It was by now 1978 and a parcel of land of some thirty acres had come up for auction on the Feock road. I was in crown court that day and left a bid with the auctioneer. When I returned I found that my bid had been accepted. I put up field shelters and moved the horses across and rented a bungalow nearby until such time as applying for planning permission on the land.

Monday was the court day for Truro magistrates to sit and on one particular Monday I walked from the police station to the city hall where the court was situated with Chippy. As usual he was smoking his pipe. We entered the court, checked that our accused were there and then sat in court. The first case was dealt with and as the next case was being called, I could smell smoke, but on glancing round I saw nothing. Suddenly, Chippy jumped up and, uttering "bloody hell," shot out of the court's side door. After a while he returned through the same door, bowed to the magistrates and took his seat next to me. "What was all that about?" I asked.

"Bloody pipe set my pocket on fire," was his reply.

"You forgot to bow to the magistrates when you left."

Opposite Truro station was a small general store which on a Sunday was looked after by a young chap who lived behind the police station. It gave the owner a day off on Sunday and the young chap, who was a tin miner, a bit of extra cash for his family. I used to pop in the shop on a Sunday for a paper so he knew me reasonably well during the time he worked there. One Sunday, I bought my paper us usual and at about lunch time, I had a call from the general office to say that the chap from the shop opposite was downstairs and wanted to see me. I took him up to the office and could see immediately that he was very agitated. I told him to take a deep breath and tell me what the problem was. What he told me was that he had been married three times but had never gone through a divorce. His first and second wives didn't have any children but he had two with his third wife. I told him that he wasn't actually married to his third wife because the second and present marriages were bigamous. I went through all the procedure with him and bailed him. He then asked if I would accompany him to his home to tell his wife as he was afraid to do so. This I did and it went off reasonably well. He later appeared in court and got probation, so he was extremely lucky.

In west Cornwall there operated a lone solicitor who took delight in representing the criminal fraternity on legal aid and would always try to outsmart police officers. When in the witness box, one of his pet things was to ask to see the constable's notebook and once having it in his possession would try his hardest to dissemble the evidence.

On one occasion, I was giving evidence on a not guilty plea in crown court in which the solicitor was aiding the barrister representing the accused and, as I expected, my pocket book was called for. The court usher passed it to the defence team and I watched as the solicitor thumbed through it and then pointed something out to the barrister followed by something whispered. The barrister said, "Officer, there appears to be a period of ten minutes not accounted for in the evidence you have given this court, when interviewing the accused. Can you tell the court what happened in those ten minutes?"

"I would rather not say Your Honour."

The barrister said, "I insist that you do."

"I would rather not say, Your Honour."

The barrister looked at the judge and the jury had now perked up as here was a detective sergeant refusing to answer the question. The judge, after the pleading look from the barrister, said, "You will answer the question, Detective Sergeant."

"Very well, Your Honour. For those missing ten minutes I was discussing the accused's previous convictions with him."

I could see the solicitor's mouth drop open and at that moment he realised the tables had been turned and I had caught him. The jury now knew that the accused had convictions and was found guilty as charged.

Several months later, the same solicitor left his wife for a younger woman and demanded that someone from the police station be in attendance when half of the goods from the marital home were being removed by a local firm. I took one of the lads from the office and went to the solicitor's former marital home. His wife was in the garden and called out for no one to worry as her husband was going to get half of everything. The furniture lorry arrived but there was no sign of the solicitor. I parked a little way up the road to watch, only really to make sure the solicitor, if he turned up, didn't cause a breach of the peace. As everything was brought out of the house, the solicitor's wife stood in the garden with a very large axe which she used to cut everything, plates and furniture alike, in half. At the same time she called out, "He wanted half of everything and now he is going to get it." She insisted that the removal men load all the smashed stuff into their lorry and sent them on their way.

That evening, the solicitor rang to complain that the police did nothing to prevent the damage, but really he didn't have a leg to stand on, or should I say, a chair to sit on!

It was now 1978 and Chief Constable Alderson had visited Truro police station and I met him as he did a tour of the station. In conversation, horses came up in connection with the cavalcade in which the Birmingham mounted horses had taken part. I mentioned also having stabled Red Rum for a couple of nights. Mr Alderson then talked about the course he had attended at Imber Court when he was a deputy assistant commissioner, as he had to learn to ride for various parades. Mr Alderson then went on to say how nice it would be to have some form of mounted section within the force area. Perhaps if I was interested it could be started with using specials and then possibly a regular section with government approval. I was asked to think it over and then ring his secretary with an answer. If it was positive, then I would have to consider a move to Exeter. When the chief constable departed, I sat down and considered what had been suggested. I knew that the government had brought in new legislation that permitted serving officers to purchase time spent in the cadet and national services to count towards their pension. I worked out that I would be able to leave with pension in 1983, having then completed twenty-seven years' service.

I had been satisfied as a detective sergeant as it gave me

the freedom of being very much hands on. The thought of being an armchair detective in the next rank never appealed to me. To be efficient in crime detection, you had to be at the sharp end continually. On two occasions in the past year I had been called to another division to take over from a man promoted from uniform sergeant to detective inspector, who on those occasions was out of his depth. I would say though, that if I had a family with children to support, then I suspect my feelings towards promotion would have been somewhat different and I would have had to climb the ladder.

I discussed what the chief had said that evening with Joy and made the decision to move to Exeter, knowing in the back of my mind that if it came to it I could retire within a short time.

I rang the chief's secretary the next day and agreed to take up the position. I told the CID staff what I was going to do. They didn't believe me until seeing the written order come through.

Joy expressed her desire to move as well and we commenced house-hunting and eventually bought a rather nice house called Ayshmeade, with two fields and a barn that I was able to convert into stabling in the village of Samford Peverell.

Within a couple of weeks, I found myself at Imber Court, the Metropolitan Police Horse Training Centre.

My measurements for the mounted uniform were telephoned through to the tailors but someone got the instructions wrong and instead of getting straight sided breeches, mine came with wings as per World War I. I immediately put the tailor right but had no option but to wear the winged breeches on the first day. On this particular day, an advanced course of officers from various forces were lined up in the indoor arena. I entered with my troop leading our horses and as I got near to the centre, a Yorkshire voice boomed out from the advanced rank, "It's a bloody good job he's holding on to that horse, or he'd fly away." The man was Barry from Yorkshire and we went on to become good friends.

I enjoyed my time at Imber Court and met some very interesting people and rode some good horses. The air though never seemed as fresh as Cornish air and I swear I heard the birds cough instead of singing as they did in Cornwall.

On most of my daily rides, we were at some stage ordered to quit and cross our stirrups for five or ten minutes to improve our balance. On the course was Frank, who had been sent by one of the African countries to learn mounted procedure and then on returning to the country, take over a mounted section. Most of the horses behaved well on the quit and cross apart from one particular horse that we all had to ride. As soon as quit and cross was ordered and we went into a canter, this horse would start to buck and no matter how good a rider you were – you came off.

On this particular day Frank was riding this rodeo horse. The order came to quit and cross which everybody did apart from Frank. The instructor called out, "Frank, quit and cross."

"No."

"Frank, quit and cross."

"No."

The instructor, now getting frustrated as we all still cantered around the arena, called out, "Frank, I'm the instructor – quit and cross."

"I'm chief inspector in my force so I am higher rank – no quit and cross."

Frank was not going to be thrown off for anyone.

Having completed all aspects of the mounted section, I now returned home. We had a couple of young thoroughbreds and Joy's riding horse called Beau. A police cavalcade was to be held in Exeter with horses from the Bristol force. The chief constable wanted me to parade with the Bristol section so I took my grey gelding, a four-year-old 16' 2" whose stable name was Grey, to Bristol and stabled him with the Bristol horses. I commuted from Samford Peverall to Bristol each day.

I had acquired Grey by coming across him in a field outside Truro when I was searching for stolen property. He was six months old and looked very poor in the corner of a small field. I traced the owner and was informed that the colt had been taken back in connection with a bad debt. I offered to buy him to clear the debt of £135. It was 1975.

Returning to my time at Bristol mounted stables, I was made very welcome and enjoyed riding out and crossing the suspension bridge, on which Grey behaved quite well apart from one time when the bridge moved slightly and he then came off his front feet but landed us both safely.

The cavalcade day arrived and it was a fine, sunny day. This was Grey's first time on parade and as we set off we had the police band in front of us and the motorcycle group behind so there was plenty of noise for the young horse to get used to. I was proud of him.

For several months I worked from home taking Grey to various functions, one of which was the opening of a new indoor school and Hanoverian stud on Bodmin Moor, connected to Trago Mills. It was a three day event with evening performances. A Horse of The Year type show with all sorts of horses present.

When I arrived, last minute preparations were being made with a lot of paint still being applied. I was allocated a stable and put him away for the night. The next morning when I arrived, I was looking not at my grey boy but a zebra. It appeared the black paint on the stable bars was still a bit tacky when I put him away the previous evening and during the night he had leant on the bars, giving him stripes. It took me about three hours to get my police horse back to his proper colour.

One morning back at Ayshmede, whilst sorting out stables, a patrol car swept into the yard. "You the chap that does horses?" asked the motor patrol driver.

"Yes," I replied.

"We've got a horse box overturned on the motorway near the Devon-Somerset border. Can you help?"

I established it was a Land Rover and trailer that had overturned with a pair of event horses inside. I hitched my Land Rover onto my horse trailer and followed the patrol car up the hard shoulder to the scene.

Traffic in all three north-bound lanes had already backed up for several miles.

On arrival it was a sad sight, with the horse box on its side in the centre lane with the two horses still inside. The Land Rover driver, a young man, had overtaken vehicles on the inside lane and in doing so the trailer had started to sway, which he couldn't control and it therefore overturned. The driver had pulled the ramp of the horse box down to try and get the horses out but one had kicked back and broken the man's leg. He was now sitting on the roadside waiting for an ambulance. The two women owners of the horses had been some distance behind the trailer in a car and were now at the scene. The patrol car officers were now getting the traffic to pass through the outside lane. I managed to get a rope on the horse lying on its side on top of the division separating the horses and, with help, pulled it out and then by the same method got the second one out. By some miracle, neither of them were injured and when taken to the hard shoulder immediately started grazing from the verge. I lowered my ramp and got both women owners to lead the horses up into the box. It worked far better than anticipated.

I then drove the horses and owners to their Torquay home. Some while later I had a nice letter of appreciation and a gift for Grey.

When we moved up to Devon, we had a couple of rescued meat rabbits of the large white variety and I built a run and hutch for them in the garden, but as rabbits do, they made an escape tunnel and spent most of their time rummaging in the stables. One morning I found the doe dead in the pen and it was sad to see the buck trying to lift her up, not understanding that she was dead. He later gave up and wandered off to the stables, which gave me a chance to bury her. From then on, Harvey (the buck's name) would take himself off across the field and sometimes would cross the road to the Tiverton canal tow path. Each evening I would go out and call him and, believe it or not, he would always come back to be secured for the night in the stables.

One winter's evening, I called and searched high and low for him but could find no trace. I returned to the house having decided to search a bit later in the hope that in the meantime he would return.

After about half an hour, the telephone rang and a man from the next village was on the line. He explained he was driving home with his wife and two children when he spotted a white rabbit in the road. They stopped and picked him up and took him home. They had made enquiries and discovered it was the policeman's rabbit from Ayshmede. He went on to say that his children, a boy and a girl aged nine and ten, had fallen in love with him. I said I would collect Harvey in the morning. I remember it was a Saturday and as I drove up the drive of the house where Harvey had been taken, I saw a young girl holding him and her brother feeding him. They had certainly fallen for him. After promising me they would give him lots of love and freedom and permission from their parent, Harvey had a new home.

Harvey hadn't quite left us because at times we would catch sight of wild rabbits in the fields with quite a lot of white on them.

One fine morning, I was exercising Grey as usual and I was in full uniform. I decided to try a different route from Sandford Peverell and crossed over the motorway heading for the village of Uffcombe. As I entered the village, parked on the nearside of the road was a builder's lorry in which sat two men having a mid-morning crib break, the driver reading a newspaper. As I drew level with the lorry, I said good morning, which was acknowledged by the driver who added, "I thought all police horses were in London."

"Oh, I'm just on holiday."

"Fair enough," he said, and carried on reading his paper.

The Tiverton canal ran a few hundred yards from the Ayshmede fields and a water run-off from the canal passed through the fields providing drinking water for the animals. I was amazed one day after a sudden downpour to find live trout in the fields having come down the run-off from the canal.

On a sadder note, I was out exercising one day when I was stopped by a local lady and gent who had been walking on the tow path and come across a large fox struggling at the end of a wire gren. I rode to where I had been directed and it was exactly as had been described. There was no way to get near it to release it, so I returned home and got my gun and put it out of its misery. I had a rough idea who may have set the trap and went to see the man. He didn't admit setting the wire but from his demeanour, I left with no doubt that it was him. There were no further traps set as far as I was aware.

I visited several shows representing the constabulary. One such show was at Oakford where, as I was unloading Grey, the riders and hounds of the local hunt tore past on their way to the main arena. Grey got excited and put on a good display of dancing on the spot. As I tried to control him, he obviously thought he should have been in that group.

Long-suffering Joy always came with me when she wasn't at her work, always making sure my uniform was brushed, as grey horse hairs on black uniform don't blend.

The time came when I thought I needed to find out whether there was going to be finance to support a mounted section. After discussion with the deputy chief constable, as the chief constable was in America at that time, it was obvious there would be no government money for funding the mounted section. I was asked what I wanted to do, and

I opted for a return to Cornwall as I knew that in a matter of months I could retire.

I retired in 1983 and on the first day of retirement commenced work as an animal health inspector for Cornwall County Council.

A few days after my retirement I was asked by the head of my department at County Hall to visit a town in west Cornwall where it was alleged a cockney fellow, who had recently moved into the area, had purchased some calves locally and had kept them in his back yard. Apparently, according to neighbours, one or more of the calves had died and the owner had stuffed their remains down a drain in his backyard, resulting in a blockage and stench. It was unknown if there were any other live animals in the yard as the man was refusing entry to the RSPCA and other local council officials.

I drove to the address to find not only the RSPCA and local council officials but a panda car with two constables who were unknown to me.

I introduced myself and was informed that the man had locked his back door, refusing to let anyone in and stating he had a shotgun.

I walked up to the back door and banged on it, getting the man's attention. I said, "I understand you will not let anyone in and you have a shotgun."

He shouted back, "Yeah, that's right."

I said, "I too have a shotgun and unless you unlock the door and come out, I'm going to blow the lock off."

The door was opened very quickly and a young man in his twenties stepped out. I said, "Have you a gun?"

He replied, "No."

"That makes two of us! Now, this is Cornwall and we don't tolerate nonsense, you will now co-operate with these other gentlemen. If you fail to do so, then I am quite sure the constables will have something to say."

The council officials and RSPCA inspector took over and I started to walk away towards my car, and as I passed the two constables, the panda driver spoke to me and said, "I just said to my mate here that if you had tried to get in the police, you would have been a good copper."

I smiled, got into my car and drove off...